Intelligent, informative and an incredible talent. Mike is the best...
next to me!

Michael Reagan

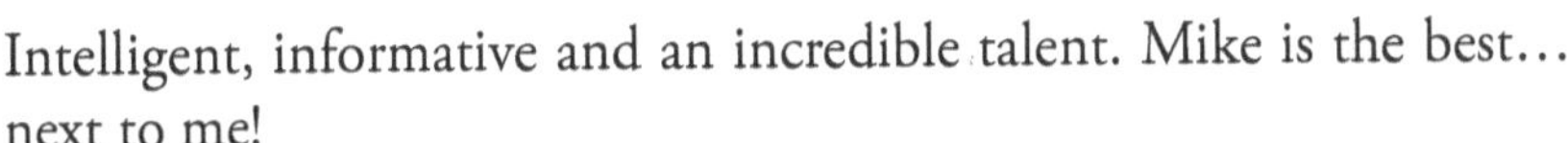

Mike Siegel is a very sweet and very talented guy...a real radio professional. I enjoy listening to Mike on the radio as I drive home from my office in the evening. His natural curiosity makes his show very entertaining and unique.

Gloria Allred

Mike Siegel has the uncanny ability to span the gamut between political aliens and space aliens. This fascinating host has had a remarkable and entertaining career in talk radio.

Alan Colmes

AIRING THE WAVE

Talk Radio At The Dawn Of The Digital Era

MIKE SIEGEL

with Stan Emert

PAGE PUBLISHING, INC.
New York, NY

First originally published by Page Publishing, Inc. 2016

ISBN 978-1-68348-336-6 (Paperback)
ISBN 978-1-68289-737-9 (Digital)
ISBN 978-1-68289-738-6 (Hardcover)

Printed in the United States of America

To Edna Siegel, a mother who cared perhaps too much and who gave me unqualified love throughout my life. Thank you, Mom, for any accomplishments I have made.

To Jack Siegel, a father who passed away too quickly and who I miss to this day. I know you are watching over me and thank you for instilling in me the values that have been so important in my personal and professional life.

Mike Siegel

To my parents, Stan Sr. and Joanne, who showed me the importance of lifetime education.

To my dear friend Dr. Lester Sauvage, who is a shining example of success through perseverance.

And finally, to my wonderful children, Brandon, Katherine, and Abigail, who *are* the future.

Stan Emert

CONTENTS

FOREWORD

The decade that followed the repeal of the Fairness Doctrine in 1987 was a transitional period in the evolution of modern media and a magical time for talk radio.

It was a bridge between the gatekeeper-controlled 20th century world of radio, television, newspapers, and magazines…and the wild, free-wheeling, democratized digital media of the 21st century.

The post-war baby boomers were coming of age. They were re-focusing their interests from rock 'n' roll, video games and youthful idealism to politics, economics, family-raising, and to a growing degree, sports.

They were becoming increasingly disgruntled with anything "big"—big government, big business, big religion, and big media.

Meantime, by the late-eighties, AM radio was falling upon increasingly hard times facing insurmountable competition from the higher fidelity music presentation of FM stereo and the resulting loss of interest in the static-ridden band by the new generation of young media consumers. It was reaching the point that many young folks didn't even know what AM was and seldom visited that side of their radio dial.

If "freedom's just another word for nothing left to lose," AM station owners began to think about an emerging, adventurous brand of *talk* radio as a viable alternative to their fading music formats. Music no longer sounded good on AM radio…but the spoken word of the human voice still came across quite effectively.

And the baby boomers—with growing interest in what was happening in the real world—already knew how to use the AM dial to which they had grown up as listeners.

Add to that the fact that without a Fairness Doctrine to repress controversial, opinionated discussion on the public airwaves, the stage was set for something vital, dynamic and "edgy" to take root.

The unique brand of talk radio that emerged during this period was the product of a far less consolidated and corporate broadcasting industry than we have today. It was less partisan and far more populist. It was even less political—at least from the perspective of being wonky—and far more general, more sociological. It was less formatted and more organic. Hosts were unique individuals, sometimes curmudgeonly, often unpredictable. They were great story-tellers. They distrusted politicians and power-seekers from all ends of the spectrum and both sides of the isle.

The groundbreaking hosts of the day were also muckrakers, watchdogs and investigative reporters who stood up to bullies on both the local and national levels. They set the agenda, rather than play follow the leader.

Mike Siegel was one such talk show host. A lawyer by training and a curious media-freak, Siegel rose to prominence as a passionate voice of the people. He was a relentless foe of corruption, greed and injustice and stands out among the best of the pack as the quintessential practitioner of the talk radio arts during what can truly be described as the genre's golden era.

In this marvelous memoir of his early life and front-line experiences in talk radio broadcasting, Siegel paints a picture and chronicles an important story about the times leading up to the seismic shift in media and attitudes marking life in our modern, emerging digital era.

Michael Harrison
Publisher, Talkers Magazine

PROLOGUE

Writing an autobiography can be the result of an inflated ego; or it can be a sharing of experiences that might make for an entertaining read or maybe have some value for the reader.

Over the years, it seems like my life has been one adventure after the other. There was not much time to "stop and smell the roses." As I have begun to think about these life adventures, I suddenly realized that I wanted to put pen to paper and have a catharsis in writing about these experiences.

The result is this book. It starts with my childhood with I formulated the interest and passion for radio. Even now I am not sure where this desire came from, but it was the focus of many of my decisions in my early years and moving forward. I hope you too will see that evolution and process and maybe be a catalyst for you to think about your own growth from childhood to your adult years.

As I entered college and the work force, my focus was communication. I also had a deep interest in the law and pursued that field as well, since the combination of communication and law was an ideal fit for me. In fact, I figured that using the law on the air would be one step ahead for me when dealing with public issues and the impact of the law on those issues.

As an example, as I write this prologue to update the book, we have the Donald Trump proposal to temporarily bar all Muslims from entering the United States. There have been intense and passionate debates about that question as to whether it is constitutional to implement this proposed policy. Having a legal background is helping me in discussing and analyzing this issue on my programs presently.

I describe my experiences laid out in this book as adventures because it seems as though my life has gone through waves of challenges, opportunities and experiences that fit this description. I would not trade these adventures for any other life. There has been so much richness in my growth and passion for life because of these ongoing life changes.

I was fortunate to enter talk radio when I did, since we had the Fairness Doctrine removed and talk hosts could opinionate without fear of reprisal from the Federal Communications Commission. It meant that hosts such as Jerry Williams (a legend in Boston), Barry Gray (the earliest talk host based in New York) and the most successful radio talk host in the history of the field, Rush Limbaugh could opinionate without restraint about public issues and public and political figures.

I was fortunate to be a small part of this era, and in fact, I remember when I was hosting at WMCA in New York in 1988, I heard Rush Limbaugh's first syndicated talk show and realized he was take our industry to a new and heightened level.

I would be remiss if I did not mention the legendary hosts from whom I learned so much over the years in just having conversations with them These include Bruce Williams, Jim Bohannon, Larry King, Rush Limbaugh, Jerry Williams, Barry Gray, Neil Rogers, Lars Larson, Michael Medved, Barry Young, Gene Burns, and others who I have been privileged to know in my adventures through the field of talk radio.

I also want to express a special thank you to a friend and colleague who has always taken the time to guide and mentor me through the intricacies of talk radio since 1989. That is Michael Harrison, Publisher of Talkers Magazine. My professional life is better thanks to Michael.

Talk radio basically saved AM radio as FM was becoming the dominant force in the audio medium. It was a time in which we flourished and enjoyed success beyond expectation during that period. Then consolidation began after President Clinton signed a Communication Act allowing broadcasters to own as many stations as they wished. The previous cap on ownership was no more.

That led to more syndication, less local programming and efficiencies becoming the decision-making factor, rather than the programming itself.

This also led to Program Directors being asked to program 2, 3 or even 4 radio stations in their market to save management costs. This meant spreading the program director thin and making the quality of each station's product susceptible to compromise.

While this was happening, we had the boom of new technology, social media, smart phones and tablets. This led to people spending their leisure time listening or watching on these devices and less attention was paid to terrestrial radio.

Those of you in your 20's or 30's no doubt rely heavily on your smart phone or tablet for news, sports and information and less on radio. Ask yourself how many radios are even being offered by retailers today?

This era was further compounded by the economic collapse of the economy in 2007 and 2008. That led to reduced revenues in the broadcast field and issues for some companies to simply survive the downturn.

It has really been a ride and I love every minute of it. That is why I call my life experiences adventures and I truly hope you will have an adventure as you read this book. Thank you for doing so.

THE EARLY YEARS

A good citizen should take his stand where
the public authority marshals him.

—Thomas Jefferson, 1790

You hear people talking about living a dream life, and you wonder if it's really true. I'm one of those lucky ones who's living a life of dreams.

But it has taken hard work, perseverance, and above all else, patience. I've lived in five cities, worked at eight broadcast stations, and guest-hosted for thirty more stations and networks. My life in media brought me in contact with presidents, international war criminals, people granting dying children one last wish, and white supremacists. I've interviewed thousands of people, given a voice to tens of thousands more, and provided a forum for peoples' cares and concerns.

Whether I'm in Boston, Miami, Nashua, Seattle, or hosting a national show, I've found that the issues of importance to people are very similar. But too many people have a national feeling of powerlessness. As we move into an age where our voices are heard internationally, it will be interesting to find if that feeling of powerlessness is universal.

Yet a group of committed people, even when starting with only two voices, becomes a driving force for change. The human condition is forever improved when people act together to right wrongs.

I know this from experience. In Boston we participated in an international campaign to end apartheid in South Africa. In Miami, we stopped a cruel phone-rate change that would have crippled senior citizens' ability to communicate. In Washington State, we exposed the nation's worst abuse of parents wrongly accused in child sex rings.

Nationally we held a new tea party to stop a whopping 51 percent congressional pay raise. We also caused a multinational oil company to account for horrendous environmental damage it caused and changed a federal law to assure such damage never takes place again.

My experience in broadcasting has provided me several cities that I can call home. Some may claim that I've had a vagabond existence having worked in so many markets. I'm proud though that industry pros have long told me that if I do truly great talk radio, I would be at many stations in my career. That's the price of being a professional in activism and communications and always pushing the envelope.

As I said, it's a dream life, and I can hardly wait for tomorrow's show. But long before my producer says "You're on!" here's how it all came to be.

Radioman

Just across the Hudson River from Manhattan lived the Siegel family in the town of Fair Lawn, New Jersey. I was a precocious but focused teenage boy who wanted to be a radioman. That was my childhood term for announcers.

By the time I was twelve, I wanted to learn how to become a radioman. Equipment was expensive. There weren't any radio stations in a box or Mr. Microphone in the late 1950s like there are today. So I saved money from my paper route and bought a Pentron reel-to-reel recorder. It was one of those oversized heavy decks. It looked like Uniblab on *The Jetsons* cartoon.

The Pentron was probably more than a kid that age should want or have, but I wanted to start out right. It retailed for $350 at the time, and I was able to get it for $230. I've always been proud of negotiating a good deal—seems I started young.

It seems like only yesterday that I brought the Pentron home. It was a Saturday in the late fall. The Jersey sky was threatening rain. I grabbed my younger brother, Victor, who is now retired from his position as auditor for a multinational charitable foundation, to help me carry this monstrosity in the house.

We set in up in the middle of the room, almost throne-like. I looked upon it with reverence, flipped the switch, and transformed myself into the radioman of my dreams. My imagination flourished.

"Welcome, ladies and gentlemen, to Mike at the Mike," I screamed into the mike. Victor giggled the laugh of a child but was always a big supporter. Sometimes I would introduce myself Sufferin' with Siegel. I imitated a DJ telling the listeners that the next song was from Elvis or Jerry Lee Lewis. Victor would play the records, holding his hands on the turntable on the 45s, and it would start just like it did on real radio. I would stop talking, and the record would begin, so we hoped.

But playing music wasn't enough. It had to sound like a real radio station. I had already researched magazines to get copy for ads. The copy became the commercials in between the songs I used to get a feel for real radio. It also gave my brother a break which, in spite of his enthusiasm, he appreciated.

I would even give the weather reports and news. The weather… well, I normally made it up. As for the news, I read it from the newspaper. As I was delivering the news of the day, I was learning current events of local interest. Little did I know at that time how important this zest for news and current events would be to me.

Victor and I had a great time! We kept our same operation for a few months, and I suddenly realized that it wasn't going to be much fun to just play records and talk for a little bit between the tunes. My interest moved much more to what was happening in the world—along the line of news.

Around the Siegel home, we used to talk about civil rights, labor rights, the environment, education, and all the issues of the day. My father was very opinionated and made his points with boisterous exuberance. But my mother's voice carried just as far. She didn't reach the highest decibel level, but she was very effective. My New York–area Jewish parents provided a haven, albeit a vociferous one, for exchanging ideas.

This made me become interested in many issues of the day. After all, I needed more material for the show! As a teenager around the age of fifteen, I started requesting to be on the mailing lists of some very strange places for a kid. Two of these were the embassies of China and Taiwan. In those days, Chiang Kai-shek was still the government leader in Taiwan, and there was a lot of rhetoric in those materials about how terrible the regime of the People's Republic of China was and how great Chiang Kai-shek was.

Whether it was the atmosphere of my home or innate curiosity, I don't know. I couldn't get enough information about events abroad. I received material from the German embassy and other embassies that gave me the opportunity to get involved and become knowledgeable about the issues. It was much more than any type of my own travelogue. It was the news!

The year was 1960, a telling time in broadcasting. The Kennedy-Nixon presidential campaign marked the first time that savvy and image communicated via radio, and television played a substantial role in choosing our next president. Whether you were politically involved or not, you couldn't escape the news of the campaign. JFK became a big inspiration to me and heightened my interest in public issues. More than that, I got involved. I took it on myself to talk to as many people as I could about John Kennedy, to tell them all how he inspired me, and to be a one-man campaign crew. The entire 1960 election experience molded my thoughts that the medium of radio could be a way to extend issues to the public doorstep. It was a vehicle to get something done about a citizen concern.

In any case, in those days I was mostly focused on news rather than talk radio because whatever talk radio I could find was folksy, chatty, not action oriented. By reading all those materials I received from around the world, I found hot spots among the Cold War. I wanted to help take action.

One day, when I was a fourteen-year-old ninth grader, I was home sick from school. I was kind of flipping the dial and found this station at 1430 on the AM dial. It was WNJR in Newark, an African-American station that played rhythm and blues and gospel. It had a high energy, soulful, and intense sound. I loved it. So it became my favorite station. To this day, R&B and gospel are my favorite music.

Announcer of Tomorrow

A couple of years later, when I was sixteen, the station ran what's called the Announcer of Tomorrow contest sponsored by Aunt Jemima, the pancake mix. So I entered and went to the studio in Union, New Jersey, just outside of Newark. My father drove me, and I read the script they provided over the air, which was material they wanted the contestants to read. My father's support played a big role in me taking the risk to extend myself. The winner of the contest would be chosen by a public vote.

Since the choice of the winner was in the citizenry's hands, I put a little article in our local newspaper, the *Fair Lawn News*, saying that I had entered this contest. If people wanted to vote for me, they could send a note to the station. Believe me, the station was happy for the free publicity. And it also taught me an early valuable lesson you need in radio—self-promotion.

Whether it was the article or my announcing, it worked! I won the Announcer of Tomorrow contest! I received a few prizes and notoriety and became sort of a station junkie. I had a radio by my bed with the station set on WNJR. I carried a pocket transistor and walked around with it pressed against my ear, sort of a mini boom box.

But the highlight during that time was on Sundays when my dad would take me to the station. I just hung out and learned by observation. A guy by the name of Pat the Cat was a weekend DJ there. He seemed to enjoy having an apprentice, and we became friends. His real name was Pat Connell. Switchin' in the Kitchen was his on-air persona. He later became a staff announcer on CBS television, the person with the big voice you would hear saying, "This is the CBS Television Network."

Maybe Pat let me stick around the station because my father would bring a whole bunch of fried chicken so we would have something to eat. Or maybe Pat liked having a loyal fan. Anyway, I was a committed groupie and didn't even know what that term meant.

I also got to know another DJ named Bill "the Burner" Mercer. He taught me a lot about the business of radio as well as on-air work. Bill discussed the importance of working with sponsors. You would think that would be natural, but it isn't. Years later I used that knowledge in helping advertisers get the best value for their dollar in presenting commercials to the listening audience.

At about the same time, I started listening to WWRL (World's Wisest Radio Listeners), another African-American station covering New York. A guy named Hal Jackson was the morning DJ there. He later became the host of Miss Black America on television every year. He had a guest DJ section. One morning a month he would have people come in and cohost the program with him. So I wrote in and asked to be a guest DJ. Sure enough, I got accepted and was scheduled from 5:30 a.m. to 9:00 a.m. I even had to get special permission from school to be late that day. That made the thrill even greater!

It was just playing singles. All I can say is that it was great. My aunt and uncle lived in Bayside, Queens, less than two miles from WWRL. So I stayed with them the night before, and my uncle was willing to get up and drive me to the studio. He waited there for me. I remember introducing "Boom Boom" by the John Lee Hooker, one of his great hits. I was fortunate enough to get to interview him in 1978 at the Gardner Dump, an outdoor concert in Gardner, Massachusetts. Now whenever I hear that song, it brings back memories of when I introduced it at WWRL.

But I knew then I didn't want to spin records. I was too interested in the issues of the day. I wanted to make a difference. When

I would talk about citizen concerns with the DJs, I was surprised to discover that they didn't seem knowledgeable about politics, government, or everyday issues the public cared about. They seemed to only want to make sure the next song was cued and they got out of the station on time.

This attitude wouldn't allow the potential of radio as a communications and information vehicle to really happen. I loved the radio-station atmosphere and still do. There's a freshness, an excitement that comes from being at the point of discussion of everything new. Cuing records just didn't cut it for me.

Kuenn for Colavito

One summer night when I was fifteen, I was at WNJR with a friend named George Grappman. Jocko Maxwell, the sports director and an on-air personality, was another person who would talk with me about broadcasting. Jocko was doing his sports news and talk show. George and I were in the control room behind the thick glass when all of a sudden Jocko burst into the room during a break.

"Come on in," he said. "I want to ask you a question on the air!"

It took us both by surprise, but I was a sports nut. I started to rush in, but George was reluctant. No matter. I grabbed him by the shirt, and we quickly followed Jocko behind the mike.

The question was what we thought of the "Harvey Kuenn for Rocky Colavito" trade. Colavito had been with the Cleveland Indians, Kuenn with the Detroit Tigers, and the teams made a straight-up trade. They were two of the great players in baseball at the time. Kuenn hit for a high average, and Colavito was a home-run hitter. It was a big deal in the major leagues. I came up with a spontaneous answer about how Cleveland was going to get a great spray hitter, and Detroit could use Colavito's power. They would both contribute positively to the mix for their new ball clubs.

This brief answer to a sports question—insignificant to most—has stayed with me all these years. The point for me was being able to immediately address the issue. The spur of the moment was then and still is the thrill of radio.

The rest of my high school years were uneventful. I continued to visit area radio stations, learning about broadcasting. The education was through osmosis, and I was happy to let it all sink in.

Fear of the Drill Instructor

After high school I went to Paterson State College in Wayne, New Jersey. My major was speech and dramatic arts. I took acting and theater classes and oral interpretation of literature classes. Those were courses as part of the major that would help develop communications skills.

Ironically, in my first semester, I was so nervous going into this speech class that I cut it for about six weeks and hung out at a gas station my friend owned. I would pump gas because I was afraid to go to class. The woman who taught the speech class had been an officer in the navy and was a stocky 6' 2", very heavy, big all over, and domineering with a capital *D*. I saw visions of her as a military drill instructor instead of a college teacher. So it really wasn't the class I feared. I thought to myself, "Maybe if I don't show up, nobody would notice."

No such luck. The school finally called me, "Mr. Siegel, what are you doing? Are you coming to class or not?" I chose the only action I could, a withdrawal failing. My first speech class and I had failed it!

I took the class over the next semester with another instructor and did very well. The rest of my college years were filled with courses geared to help me in communications. I flirted with other tracks such as political science and history for prelaw, but broadcasting was and still is my passion.

I completed my bachelor of arts in speech and communications and announced my presence to the world—only the world didn't exactly beat down my door. I searched but found only one radio audition. It was at an FM station in Pennsylvania. I did terribly and didn't land the position. That left me more discouraged than I had been as a youngster when I recorded programs in my reel-to-reel tape recorder.

I thought I needed more life experiences, and I had bills to pay. In college, I had gotten an elementary school teacher's certificate. So I decided to go into education and manned a classroom in Newark for four years.

Newark

Teaching in Newark in the late 1960s was an incredible experience. I was there during the riots and Vietnam protests of that era. I was given an occupational deferment from military service. I hadn't sought one, but when I met with the draft board, I was told, "We need good teachers in the city even more than we need soldiers." I was both relieved and surprised. I was willing to go but freely admit to being afraid of what I would face.

It was a terrible time for our country and an extremely difficult time to be a teacher in the inner city. Facing the kids every day was tough, but it wasn't the same as risking your life at every turn in Vietnam. I still lived with my parents in upper-middle-class white suburbia. My homelife and my work life gave me a great insight into disparity between how some of us live versus others.

One of the activities I did with my kids was to have them come to my home in Glen Rock on a Saturday for a barbecue. It was amazing to see the neighbors watching all my fourth graders— black kids—coming to Glen Rock. The neighbors would peer over the fence so that you could only see the tops of their heads and some of their eyes. It was easy to sense the neighbors' apprehension about what was going on, but I didn't really care because these kids were important to me.

The experience of teaching in Newark showed me the importance of being able to express a point of view. So many of these kids wouldn't speak out because they never expected anyone to listen. I tried as a teacher to hear them and help them develop a sense of power within themselves. I refuse to believe that the youthful idealism of the 1960s must vanish in favor of the personal greed we see so much as we traverse the new millennium.

I set out to change the world—or at least my little corner of it. While I was teaching at the age of twenty-three, I ran for borough council as a Democrat in Glen Rock. There was at least a two-thirds majority of Republican-registered voters. It was going to be tough, to say the least. Of course, there was racial tension during the time, but I felt that if people of different races would get to know each other as kids—play together, experience that sense of closeness that comes for kids when they get dirty together—we could start to put a dent in racial prejudice.

One of my proposals was to bring in the black kids from Paterson, an inner-city area, to be allowed to come into our city swimming pool in the summer. The pool was off-limits at that point.

My proposal, to say the least, wasn't well received. You would have thought I was asking to legalize arson as a spectator sport.

This very conservative, restrained, protected community felt threatened by four-foot-tall, eighty-pound black kids from the ghetto. But there was an element of the public who understood and agreed with what I was saying. The undercurrent of support for what I was saying spelled danger for the local power brokers. So in the stealth of night, without notice, the borough council met in private. They passed a resolution that disallowed any outsiders the use of the swimming pool.

The public mood was different then from today. It was less cynical and less prone to action. The council ordinance effectively took the issue off the table before the election. At least I had the impact of forcing them to face the issue, but because the makeup of the town being so heavily Republican, I had no chance of winning. This was the first time I had seen an elite group in charge of government act in private over a public matter. It left a bad taste in my mouth and is a lesson I've never forgotten.

For government to be of the people, by the people, and for the people, it must be open. If we truly govern ourselves, there are no secrets. Acting clandestinely in the middle of the night or in board rooms or on the golf course is not what any free society should tolerate.

With activist broadcasting deep in my heart at the time but having doubts about my future, I obtained master's and doctoral degrees in communications at Paterson State and the University of Utah. Then I returned to New England and taught communications at Fitchburg State College in Massachusetts.

During that time, in my first year at Fitchburg, I invited the program director, Michael O'Neil, from local station WEIM to come into the class to talk about radio as a communications medium. I remember listening to him talk and probably asked more questions than did my students. My passion for radio and to be involved in issue advocacy was still burning.

O'Neil recognized the blaze. He asked me after class if I had any interest in working in radio. I smiled and said, "I used to," and left it at that for the time being.

THE POWER OF TALK RADIO

To the press alone, chequered as it is with abuses, the world is indebted for all the triumphs which have been gained by reason and humanity over error and oppression.

—James Madison, 1799

Saying Yes

The brief conversation with O'Neil after he had spoken to my class was at the forefront of my mind for several days. It was flattering to me and gnawing at me at the same time. Clearly, my drive to get into radio reappeared. We chatted a few times about how the public reacted to various news programs and whether news was information or entertainment. The term *infotainment* had not yet been coined.

In late December 1972 I was at a speech communications convention in Chicago when I received an urgent call from home. I was told that Mike O'Neil offered me a Saturday news job and wanted me to start December 30.

It wasn't much money, and the time slot wasn't the best. It wasn't even talk radio—it was just news. But it didn't matter. I immediately accepted.

I returned early from the thrilling convention of academicians and prepared to start my first professional broadcast. I wanted to do the news—the events of the day—so well that I could handle any last-minute upheaval.

Thereafter, every Saturday I was live on the air with news for seven hours, and I would tape three broadcasts to air for five more hours. So on Saturdays, I was the voice of the news from 5:00 a.m. to 5:00 p.m. This was heaven!

O'Neil allowed me the freedom to be active about the news. Rather than just reading the wire service reports, I would take local stories from the morning newspaper and call some of the personalities mentioned to get actualities. An actuality is a recorded statement intended for broadcast. This raised the bar for newscasts on the station and made it sound highly professionally produced.

Then I began to fill in for the weekday talk-show host, Jack Raymond, who was still at WEIM twenty-nine years later. My first stint was for Jack's two-week vacation. Talk radio was just starting to lose its innocence and naivete. The controversies and rancor of the times reflected the deeply divided, ever-growing diverse population.

One of the first things I did as Jack's fill-in related to a Fitchburg state representative named George Bourque. I don't remember the issue, but Bourque had the ability to greatly impact the specific public policy in question. And the people were adamant. They didn't like the proposal and made their views known everywhere in the township. It was the closest thing this community had seen to an uprising in years.

Numerous calls came into the station, asking for something to be done. This was surprising to a large extent because the people were claiming to be powerless. So I told the audience, "Folks, just call Representative Bourque at his office at the statehouse in Boston. Don't let this be done to you. It's your government. You *are* the government. Let him know how you feel!" After all, they elected him, and they paid his salary, and he worked for them. The people should be able to influence their representative. I gave out the legislative office phone number.

Then something happened that had never happened there before——- or at least it hadn't occurred. A citizen revolt was underway!

Bourque got call after call from an irate public. He was amazed that he got these calls from people who had listened to the program. In fact, he was so deluged with calls he changed his mind on the issue. The people's voice had spoken loudly.

I praised the representative for being responsive to the people. But he remembered the criticism more than the praise. That too was a lesson learned that is still true today.

The Bourque campaign was the start of my lifetime challenge to hold politicians accountable in March 1973. Working with the public during that two-week period helped me realize that this was my life's calling—to explain, discuss, and encourage action on issues. And to get paid for doing what you love is everyone's dream.

Talking about and debating issues was my passion. I grew up with it at home. In my family, spirited noncontact, verbal sparring was as vicious as any prize fight in boxing. My parents' interest in the issues of the people cultivated my interest and motivation.

The Exorcist

Later in the year I was hosting interview programs on Montachusett Cable Television in Fitchburg and Leominster, Massachusetts. The movie *The Exorcist* came out, and I found it very intriguing.

I've always been fascinated with religious phenomena, and the believability of the movie was certainly hotly debated. Most people seemed to feel that the movie was total fiction and that there were no such things as exorcisms. They summed the film up as a good scary movie.

I looked into the genesis for the story of *The Exorcist*, and the name Father Eugene Gallagher appeared. It seems that he knew of his own knowledge about the reality of removing demons from the souls of people. I wasn't sure of my own level of belief, but this was too interesting to not proceed further.

The cable television program had no budget for travel and investigation. But since I was also director of advertising, I took my initial findings to a local bank to fund a trip to Philadelphia to interview Father Eugene Gallagher. The bank president agreed. We had a sponsor who wanted to find out if *The Exorcist* was real!

Father Gallagher was agreeable to talking with me on camera. In 1949, one of his students in a philosophy of religion class was William Peter Blatty, the author of *The Exorcist*.

Apparently, Blatty learned his lessons well and later wrote to Father Gallagher for more information on exorcisms.

Father Gallagher and I did over two and a half hours of interviews at his church in Philadelphia. He talked about actual exorcisms. They included the case on which the book and movie was based. He personally related the story about the very petite woman from Iowa who actually vomited gallons of green liquid. There were thirty witnesses in the room at the time. There were eyewitnesses to levitation off the bed. These eyewitnesses also reported it took several strong men to bring the bed back down.

Father Gallagher talked about a case in the early 1950s in Mount Rainier, Maryland, where a thirteen-year-old boy was apparently possessed. The boy was spewing out Latin, a language he did not know, and somehow immediately gained enormous physical strength.

The boy's family had gone to the local priest after medical doctors and psychologists could not solve the problem. Eventually, the boy was sent to a seminary in Saint Louis. Several young members of the seminary came to drive the boy the nine hundred miles to Missouri from Maryland. On the evening just before arrival, the boy leaped to the front seat from the rear, grabbed the steering wheel, and swerved the car toward a steep embankment off the road. It took all four seminary students in the car with him to get the strength to pry the boy loose from the steering wheel.

Father Bowdern at the seminary performed an exorcism, and it was successful. The boy recovered, grew up, and married. Father Gallagher would not tell me the details of the exorcism itself. At the time we aired the programs, the boy had no recollection of anything that had happened to him.

The circumstances surrounding the factual basis for *The Exorcist* and about exorcisms in general have been well chronicled. The Catholic Church doesn't speak often of such events, and my purposes for undertaking the investigation and doing the programs were solely for a search for the truth.

More Lessons

A few months after the citizen education of Representative Bourque, a new program director entered. He was Bob Cohen, who has since become a very close friend. He and I later owned two radio stations (temporary licenses) in New Hampshire. He came in to tell me, "Look, I'm sorry to tell you this, but we have to cut back on expenses. Saturday news is one of the places we have to cut."

That ended my time at WEIM and was a real lesson for me to learn about radio. Since then, I've learned many times over that no matter how good the quality of the show, you can be pulled off the air for nearly any reason.

In any business, the bottom line is the bottom line, as they say. But in radio, the bottom line is a moving target. Radio is a fickle business. Regardless of this painful lesson about the lack of security in this kind of work, it will always be what I will always do. Talk radio must act as a protagonist and help the common man, the average, everyday Joe, have a voice.

My next radio job was at WLMS in Leominster, Massachusetts. I did a one-hour talk show every Saturday. The station was a music station and didn't promote my show. So I didn't get many calls. I was forced to do monologues.

It was great training but painful. I would look at the phone board and see no lights blinking and I wondered what I was going to talk about next to pique the public's interest. That also meant that I had to get to know all the issues of interest to the public. Not only that, but I had to know all sides of the local issues, including parochial nuances. You can't always know what the hot button is. So I made sure I was prepared for any discussion on any topic.

Again, the experience was a lesson. I learned to hold audience interest but sometimes had to try to put myself inside the listeners' heads to make sure the show was interesting. Even more than that, I had to keep my hand on the pulse of the community to make sure I knew what the current issues were. Out of necessity, I was quickly becoming one of the most informed citizens in the community.

From Leominster in 1975, I went to WAAB in Worcester, Massachusetts, a bigger market. The bigger market was the appeal for me because of a greater likelihood of an engaged listenership.

I did Saturdays, late afternoon and early evening programs. There was no board operator and no screener, but we did get a lot of calls. This job provided yet another important lesson in radio timing. And thank goodness for the seven-second delay, also known as the dump button. Some of the things people say weren't heard on radio because of that button and won't be printed here either.

I was so involved with all the technical aspects that I don't recall any specific issues. Sometimes I felt like a traffic cop at a busy intersection. But what I do remember is the fervor of the people to have a voice in local matters. It seemed the politicians weren't serving their constituents but some other interests instead. This definitely made for great radio.

Then one Saturday the program director, Chris Cross, called collect while I was on the air. He told me to tell the owner of the station that he was resigning. I thought it was kind of strange that he was telling a part-time talk-show host to convey this kind of message to the owner, but he had already moved.

That was easily one of my strangest moments on radio. I remember having people stop me on the street and ask about that call. All I could say was, "I have no idea what that was about." All I knew is that my boss was gone, and I had to tell the big boss.

Anyway, I called the owner, George Gray, at home, and conveyed the message. He didn't sound surprised. A few weeks later, the new program director called and said they had changed the format to music. There was no need for a talk host, but I could stay as a DJ, if I wished. The musical chairs of radio were the tune I heard again.

I went to the station that weekend supposedly to play music. I sat in the chair with the turntable by my side. I picked up the first vinyl selection and placed it over the knob holding the record in place. The music started playing, and I looked down with a blank stare on my face.

I said to myself, "Wait a minute. I can't do this. I'm not a DJ. I'm a talk host." I had to take a stand.

While the song played, I reached across the operations board and turned on the dump seven-second delay button. I told the listeners, "There are issues out there that the people want to discuss. This is radio, and it's your voice. Let's talk."

A new civic center, presumably a good project, had just been announced in the city. That wasn't the way the public saw it. The people were outraged that the center was going to be built at all. It was incredibly expensive, all at taxpayers' cost, and nearly every caller didn't believe the center was needed. I didn't know the issue all that well myself, but the people educated me, and they had their say.

The listeners knew that the station's format had changed, but they wanted their voice to be continued. The station started getting call after call. "Keep Mike Siegel" was the message that management received over and over. In fact, the station had never received that many calls about anything.

Here's another point of education about radio. Managing a talk-radio format is a hassle. The owner of the station had another primary business. Radio was almost a hobby to him. Music is easier and cheaper. Talk radio results in management receiving calls from irate citizens. And not every caller agrees with the topic. Management doesn't always agree with talk hosts' views on topics. Music rarely causes problems.

Stepping up in Boston

I got a break and moved to WBOS in Boston. Alan Temple, the general manager, was interested in the idea of a talk show. So in late 1975,

I broke into the Boston market late Sunday nights from eight o'clock to midnight. I was there for quite some time and was a success.

Forced busing to achieve racial balance was the big issue at the time. Federal judge Arthur Garrity had taken over the school system. People in South Boston were literally getting violent when African-American kids were bussed into the nearly all white schools. The people would surround the parked buses and shake them with the kids on board!

It was an explosive situation. Racial violence was something that happened in the South in the 1950s and 1960s, not in Boston. But the public didn't want busing, and they wanted a place to tell the world.

I covered this every week, and the conversation became extremely heated. I supported busing at that time because I felt there was a need to get the African-American kids into integrated class-rooms. In fact, the 1954 Supreme Court decision (Brown v. Board of Education) really said that separate cannot be equal by definition because the minority group will feel inferior to the others. I strongly believed in desegregation of public schools and let that be known to my audience. It didn't make me popular with too many politicians or the establishment of Boston, but it did allow the people to educate themselves about the issue. The important thing was to get people talking even though many of the callers vehemently disagreed with me.

Being able to disagree with people without being disagreeable or cantankerous is a skill I had from my youth. But I'm told that not everyone would agree with me about that. Yet debate and the art of persuasion through logic and passion are an equally important skill. My position on desegregation was based on my own social and academic beliefs. Many of the intense people of South Boston were very much opposed to busing. Nearly to a person, they were whites who were vehemently against having African-Americans in schools where their children went. They desperately wanted to maintain the status quo.

And they were outraged with Jerry Williams, the most popular talk host in the city, who antagonized them with inflammatory language. He made a terrible mistake in ridiculing the character of the people of South Boston. I didn't feel that was necessary and instead chose to argue the issue, not the person. Jerry's actions caused a violent reaction against him and even his wife's antique business. In fact, Jerry's wife was forced to close the business for her own safety.

The school desegregation issue in Boston showed very clearly the difference between informing and engaging about a topic and inflaming emotions without logic. Passionate dialogue based on deeply held beliefs is perfectly acceptable in radio, but foaming-at-the-mouth diatribes are not. I hold radio in such high regard that I, as a talk host, strive to encourage listeners to carefully consider all sides of the issue and then speak their minds. Radio informs. An uninformed public is dangerous to our democratic republic.

Crossing the Road

After just one year, the station changed its format to country music. Right across the street was WITS (Information, Talk, Sports). I walked in and asked for a job.

Bill Schubert, the operations manager, was glad to see me and asked, "When can you start?"

"Right away!" was the immediate and obvious answer.

I wound up doing morning drive, *Dr. Mike Siegel at the Information Desk*, from six o'clock to ten o'clock. It wasn't that much talk because of the time slot. From six to nine I did information segments, and from nine to ten I did talk radio.

One of the great issues we did was to talk about the rumor of a gas tax increase that Governor Ed King was floating. It all started the morning we had transportation officials on the air in the news hours talking about the issue. This was the ultimate "finger in the wind" determining what the public thought. I was personally offended that the governor didn't have the decency to talk with the people directly. Instead, he wanted to test it through his minions and with leaks to the press.

So from 9:00 a.m. to 10:00 a.m. I hammered at it and urged the people to call the statehouse to tell the governor what they thought.

The capitol was inundated with calls from irate citizens. And very few callers were telling the governor to raise gas taxes.

Within a few short days, the governor issued a statement saying there would be no gas tax increase proposed. This helped me realize the power of talk radio.

The station hired a comic, Emperor Hudson, to take over morning drive and moved me to evenings. The station liked the interaction and involvement of the people and felt it would be better later in the day. Management was right, and I was elated—for the moment.

Then Chris Cross (yes, the same Chris Cross) came in as program director and asked me to do overnights from midnight to 5:00 a.m.

"All night long?" I shrieked.

He asked me to think about it, especially since the nighttime signal on this AM radio station reached nearly a third of states east of the Mississippi River.

It didn't take me long. I agreed because doing an overnight show in a major city is great. We had calls from everywhere!

It may seem that I was too agreeable to make changes—too ready to comply with management's wishes. The difficulty at the time was that talk radio was not a stable format. It was, and probably still is, a personality-driven format. That means it's expensive. The better ratings and more popular a host gets, the more advertisers want to places commercials on his show. The more expensive the commercials on your show, the more money you can demand as a talk host. It is not unlike professional athletes who play on a championship team. Before you know it, the team salary is too expensive to keep all the players.

Additionally, owners have to be thick-skinned enough to take heat from local power brokers, who feel the unfettered wrath of citizens. While some hosts try to control callers, I believe talk radio should be used as a vehicle for people. Empowerment of the audience is the most effective technique for success and compelling, entertaining talk radio.

"We need to teach these criminal blacks a lesson."

In 1978 there was unrest in South Africa. Massive riots were taking place in Johannesburg. Blacks were getting killed in droves, and whites feared for their lives. Police brutality seemed to be a way of life. Our nation considered whether the United States should impose some type of sanction.

Should America help the native people? After all, South Africa was thousands of miles and an ocean away. Should Americans care? I thought they would.

One night while on the air, we dialed the police station in Johannesburg. Who better to talk to than someone right in the middle of the circumstance? I was lucky enough to get a police chief in charge of trying to hold back the riots. We talked for forty-five minutes on the air. He knew he was on the radio; there were no secrets.

One of the statements he made was incredible. It surprised me. This white South African police chief said, "We need to teach these criminal blacks a lesson." I couldn't believe what I heard and asked him to repeat it.

"We need to teach these criminal blacks a lesson!" he said louder and more emphatically.

That was an astonishing statement to make. Here was a police chief empowered to uphold the law and protect the public—all the public. But this police chief of the country's largest city by far, speaking as a representative of his government, made it obvious that racism was embedded among the controlling whites in the South African culture.

After the conclusion of the interview, I turned the rest of the show, for the next four hours, over to the callers. It was overwhelming! People said they couldn't fall asleep because to learn about what was going on firsthand was remarkable. To hear about the intensity of the racism that existed was educational, to say the least. To find that people were losing their lives because of the color of their skin took the listeners back to darker times in our own country. And the listeners weren't going to let it happen.

Action took place. One of the first callers asked, "What can we do about this?" Calling South Africa wasn't going to do any good, but the United States was one of the two superpowers in the world. Americans had a power that only the Soviets rivaled.

I believe that each American—each listener—felt pride in their country that night. When I gave out the phone numbers of area members of Congress, there was an awe-inspiring feeling that this was America at its best. Through talk radio, the people became informed and then chose to act.

In fact, the audience—everyone on this overnight show—was substantial enough to inundate the officeholders' phones. I don't know the exact impact of the show, but the public outcry around the nation caused Congress to set in motion sanctions that would show the world American humanity.

Talk radio was able to bring out into the open something that other types of media could not. The people exercised a collective voice.

HOSTAGES AND FIRINGS

The greater the power, the more
dangerous the abuse.

—Edmund Burke, 1771

"We don't want to start a war."

In 1980, there was a presidential election and a hostage crisis. Americans being held overseas was a highly charged issue, and the campaign atmosphere brought the continuing tragedy to the forefront. President Jimmy Carter, a good and decent person, was having difficulty with circumstances. Little did Carter know that the American hostages had become pawns of the campaign.

The United States had cut off relations with Iran. The national mood was one of tension. The memories of the Vietnam War were too close for comfort. The American psyche could not handle another "conflict" where the lives of thousands of mostly young men were ended.

One Friday night, my terrific, aggressive producer named Paul continuously called Tehran. One of my students at Emerson College who came to the studio often was there that night and helped make the calls too. We were determined to reach someone who would talk with us about the hostage issue from the Iranian point of view. From midnight to 4:30 a.m., Paul and the student tried to find a point of contact in Tehran.

After four and one-half hours of continuous pleas on the phone, Paul burst out of the control room into the broadcast booth and said in muffled tones, "I've got somebody. But don't upset him. We don't want to start a war."

This was truly a monumental moment because it placed the hostage crisis as close as we could get it without being there. The radio audience could almost feel the situation themselves. On the other end of the phone line was a Mr. Anginey, who worked for the Iranian government. Thank goodness he spoke English.

It turned out that Anginey was the press aide to the Ayatollah Khomeini himself. I knew we were going to get spun like a top, but at least it was direct. Anginey came on at 4:30 a.m., and I was to go off at 5:00 a.m. So I had to work quickly but carefully. My producer was right. We didn't want to exacerbate the matter. Nobody in the general public had been able to talk to anybody in Iran up to this point. It was a very tense time, and we were literally on the cutting edge of the story.

I referred to Khomeini as the Imam (holy man) to show respect and not upset Anginey. This was difficult for me because as a Jew, Anginey's country would just as soon see my people perish from the Earth. This was a new experience for me—giving a voice to someone who wanted to kill me and my family solely because of our faith.

Anginey said there were three things Iran wanted: (1) monies of the "criminal" Shah of Iran unfrozen and sent to the Iranian government; (2) the "criminal" Shah transported to Iran for trial; and (3) the United States to mind its own business and get out of Iran.

In order to get the story to the listeners, I had to have just a quiet dialogue with Anginey. Essentially, I gave him control of the microphone so that the people could hear what he had to say and decide for themselves. So many times during the interview, I wanted to break in and lambaste his government for atrocities against the people. But that wouldn't have served the audience.

It was an exciting, tense thirty minutes. In fact, we canceled all the commercials to not lose Anginey.

I wish I could have participated in the reaction of my listeners the following night. I wish we could have led a citizens' charge to demand that the government open a meaningful discussion with Iran, or maybe we should have gone to war. Either way, the American people needed to be involved to let their elected officials know how they felt.

Ironically, the interview with Anginey was to be my last show at WITS.

I received my paycheck the week before and got 60 percent less!

I called Cross, who said, "We have to make cuts."

"You didn't even tell me. I can't work for this amount of money," I said emphatically.

He said, "Fine, but that's the way it is. This next show will be your last."

Again station management was inundated with calls from an angry audience. I wanted to be talking with the people about issues, but instead the issue was me. It was not a comfortable place, but the owners pulled the strings. At least, we ended the show with a bang.

Over that weekend, I was visiting with a friend in New Hampshire, and Cross somehow got the number where I was. He said, "We need you. We're getting flooded with calls. We'll pay what we paid you before."

I agonized about it. On the one hand I was considering whether I would lose face by returning to WITS. On the other hand, what I wanted to do was to communicate and give others the opportunity to have a voice. I decided that what would help me pursue my goals would be to be back on radio. I returned to WITS.

I've already discussed the nature of the business and how insecure it is. But the upsetting thing is that it doesn't seem to matter about the quality of the show or the response of the listeners. It would seem to me to only be logical that if a show is popular with the public, then that show would be used in soliciting advertising. Yet a talk-show format is expensive due to host cost. It is highly unusual for a station to go part talk and part music. The mixed promotional costs would be too high. Mixed formats can work in small markets, but listener loyalty is extremely important in the big cities. That means that if a station owner is going to engage in talk radio, he's going to go at it all the way.

So the only way to get job security is to own your show or, better yet, own a broadcast property.

FCC Uses Both Feet

There was a station in Nashua, New Hampshire, that had gotten in operational and financial trouble. The owner started trimming, then cutting, and finally bludgeoning every corner he could. Plus, he bled his customers dry. It turned out that not all the owner's actions were legal.

This former owner, Pat Bronstein, lost the stations (WOTW AM-FM) due to fraudulent billing. Bronstein had been warned, fined, and otherwise given every opportunity to keep the license, but finally the FCC came down on Bronstein with both feet. My partner, Bob Cohen, and I went through the Commission's comparative hearing process to obtain an interim operator's license for the stations. Realistically we didn't have the money to buy the stations outright. But by getting the interim license, we forfeited the right to apply for a permanent license. Knowing that the Commission's processes were very slow at the time, we believed we would have ample time to develop the business.

We had those stations for seven years from 1978 to 1985 while the FCC went about the arduous process of finding a new owner. I was general manager for the first two years, but it was a horrendous schedule. I was often doing overnight on-the-air work in Boston. I would get home about 5:30 a.m., sleep until about noon, and then go into the Nashua station to work the rest of the day. I didn't do an on-air shift in Nashua but was just the manager. We had to keep costs as low as possible because we couldn't put capital into the business.

It was great experience, and it helped me understand the business of broadcasting a lot better.

Still, being a GM was no substitute for communicating with the people over the airwaves.

Remember Jerry Williams? He was my fellow talk host from Boston who had infuriated South Boston during school desegregation. Well, Jerry had gone to Miami at WNWS to become operations manager. He also hosted the two-to-six show in the afternoon. Jerry had been in the business for about thirty years. He knew everyone, and everyone knew him. And he knew talk radio.

My schedule of nighttimes on the air in Boston and daytimes in management in Nashua was getting to me. I ultimately left WITS when Mutual Broadcasting paid a substantial fee to get Larry King syndicated on that station doing overnights.

I called Jerry Williams just to chat. I told him about what had happened at WITS, the interim operation at Nashua, and my own long-term goals. He said that his 8:00 p.m. to midnight host, Neil Rogers, was leaving to go to a Nashville station. This was a surprise because Rogers had a good reputation, and I thought he was quite popular in Miami. But the one constant in radio is change.

The conversation with Jerry was thought-provoking and seemingly prophetic. Jerry said he would be back in touch, and I thought in the back of my mind that Miami would be an interesting place to live.

Florida Before the Vote

It wasn't too long before Jerry called back and told me, "Siegel, are you ready to come to the land of eternal sunshine?" It was too good an opportunity to pass up. I would have my own show in a great market. For me, it was a dream I'd had since playing talk-radio host many years ago with my brother.

I went through all the notifications of a job change, addresses, phones—you name it. I packed my thirteen suitcases, said good-bye to friends, hired a new GM for the Nashua station, and was ready to leave Saturday morning after Thanksgiving 1980. I love Boston. It was sad to leave but exciting to go to a new part of the country.

On Friday night before I was to leave the next day, I got a call from Jerry Williams. The call came in at 6:05 p.m. He said, "Siegel, the deal's off." I stood there with my jaw on the ground. I had already gone through huge changes. He said Neil Rogers was returning to Miami. Woody Sudbrink owned the stations in the two cities and said Rogers would be able to return.

I wasn't surprised. I predicted at the time for many reasons that Rogers and Nashville just wouldn't fit. But that didn't make it any better for me. I had made commitments to people to replace me. I had given up my place of living. To renege on all of that would not be the right thing to do. I was comfortable but not independently wealthy enough so that I didn't have to work. And I had no job.

Williams felt terrible. He should have. He asked me to move to Miami anyway, and he would do his best to get me a show. He made no promises, but he was going to try to get me on from 6:00 p.m. to 8:00 p.m. by the first of the year.

So I had to decide. Do I leave Nashua? I had just given up my life in New Hampshire. Would it be fair to fire the new GM at WOTW just because of what happened to me? Would I be totally crazy to trust anyone in broadcasting?

I chose Florida. I would take the chance. My parents had moved to the Fort Lauderdale area. I figured I could go there and spend time with my family.

Williams assured me he would get me as much fill-in as possible, but that his goal was to have me on full time by January. He kept his word. On January 5, 1981, I started full time at WNWS from 6:00 p.m. to 8:00 p.m.

CORPORATE GIANTS AND NORTHERN IRELAND

It is the misfortune of king s that they
will not listen to the truth.

Johann Jacoby, 1848

Printing Press of Cash

I couldn't believe it. A ten-month long battle was coming to a successful conclusion. There I was with Walter Dartland, a consumer advocate, at the Florida State Public Utilities Commission in a packed hall
of senior citizens screaming for justice. We'd been waging a campaign
to wrest back control of phone rates for the people.

Florida, 1981—a state made up of many elderly people, a few
of them pretty well-off financially. Most of them had long since
blazed their own trails and were in the serene twilight years of their
lives. You would think their time would be spent relaxing. But on
this day, they were rabid activists. They filled the massive auditorium

asking—no—demanding that the monopolistic, behemoth phone company listen to them.

It was on that day that the people brought Bell to its knees.

In the Sunday, January 4, 1981, edition of the Fort Lauderdale News *Sun Sentinel*, there was a story on the front page about Southern Bell's local measured service. This was a way for the phone company to charge residents on a per-minute basis for local calls. At the time, AT&T owned all the regional phone companies, including Southern Bell.

I believed that local measured service would be ridiculously harmful to the elderly, many of whom were on fixed incomes. It would have been a printing press of money for AT&T. It was something AT&T desperately wanted all over the country.

So on my first night on the air, January 5, 1981, we took on AT&T. To many, this was the first time they had heard of the proposal. I was inundated with phone calls. It was amazing to me that on this first night the people were so outraged.

It was the start of something for me that has been among my most satisfying experiences in talk radio: protecting senior citizens who trusted the phone company as if it were the government they fought for in WWII.

The callers kept repeating, "We must do something about this, but what can we do?" In a way it reminded me of the shows years before in Massachusetts with Representative Bourque. The people didn't have to be powerless.

So right in the middle of the show, we decided to start a campaign against local measured service. And what a campaign it was! We kept it going from that night, January 5, 1981, until the PUC commissioners made their decision on October 24, 1981.

We decided to wage a petition-gathering campaign. Through my program, we were able to get the signatures of 130,000 people in opposition to local measured service. The notoriety of the signature gathering itself caused Florida's Public Service Commission to hold a public hearing in Hialeah for Dade County citizens. All the commissioners attended.

We knew that each person testifying would only have a brief time to speak. We were concerned that the complete negative impacts of local measured service wouldn't get communicated. So we did something pretty dramatic. We had about thirty people waiting in line who deferred to me to testify on behalf of the people.

My charge was to talk about the fact that, as a group, the people were nearly unanimously opposed to the measure because it only benefited the phone company. Many retired people use the phone as their lifeline. It was nothing for these retirees to be on the phone with a neighbor for an hour. The personal contact permitted through telephone conversations provided that human touch so much needed by all of us. This is even more true among seniors. If they had to pay on the basis of local measured service, all local phone service would, in effect, be toll calls.

Local measured service would create great disruption to retirees, who came out in force on the issue. Their energy transferred to me, and it snowballed. Normally, PSC hearings had about ten people. Nearly six hundred people showed up that night.

I testified that we had a message for the commissioners. At that point, senior citizen after senior citizen got up and approached the podium and placed all of these thousands of petitions on the table in front of the commissioners. The pile was so high that it blocked the view of the commissioners from the rest of the room. It was almost like that famous scene in *Miracle on 34th Street*.

After digging out from under the deluge of mail, the commissioners said they appreciated receiving it. The place was near bedlam as I testified on behalf of the people. I reminded the commissioners that because they were appointed by the governor, we would hold the governor accountable if local measured phone service was adopted. The chairman, Joe Cressy, became indignant and said I was out of order. The people booed, reminiscent of what I heard at Dodger games as a youth in Brooklyn.

Cressy backed off and became more respectful of the people. They scheduled a second hearing in Broward County (Fort Lauderdale) because of the attendance at the first hearing. The show turned out the people again in Fort Lauderdale. One of my station colleagues, Al Rantel, who was on from 10:00 a.m. to 2:00 p.m., said it was too much of an uphill fight. He predicted local measured service would unanimously pass the PSC. "You can't beat Ma Bell," Al said.

The strength was in the people. At the October 24 hearing, the PSC voted unanimously to defeat local measured service. I later learned that the PSC taped every show I did, and Larry Mixon, the PR person for Southern Bell, would appear on the program for equal time purposes. He would bring transcripts of the shows and say, "Did you know that on such and such date at 6:30 p.m., on this program, you said such and such about the president of the company?"

I gave Mixon the time because it made for a good radio show. We did those periodically, and it created great audience interest. The entire campaign had an enormous life of its own because it was driven by the listening public.

About five years later, I was working at a West Palm Beach station (WJNO), and Larry Mixon was a guest on my show about consumer issues. I asked him about local measured service. He looked me in the eye and said, "When Mike Siegel supports local measured service, that's when we'll bring it back."

To this day it hasn't been brought back. I'm very gratified that we were able to defeat this anti-consumer measure.

That was a major event at WNWS. I left the station when Jerry Williams went back to Boston. My predecessor, Mike Levine, in the time slot had a 1.8 and 1.9 Arbitron ratings. I had a 4.2 in my first rating (called a book in the industry). These ratings are incredibly important for stations because they directly affect how much can be charged for commercials. Since my ratings were so much higher than others at the station, I figured that when Williams left, I would get the plum spot—afternoons, 2:00 p.m. to 6:00 p.m.

I didn't get the job. They gave it to a woman. I heard rumors they were hiring someone other than me, and I left a note under the GM's door saying that if they hired someone else for that time slot, I was going to leave. I felt I was being slighted.

They hired Shirley Peters, and it turned out it was because she was willing to take less money than just about anyone would take.

I don't blame her though. Women had a very difficult uphill fight getting talk-radio jobs in the early 1980s. So I left, which generated six hundred letters from my listeners who were distressed I was gone.

About a week later, I dropped by the station, and the GM asked me, "What did you do to me with all these letters?"

His desk was overwhelmed. We agreed I would go back on weekends. The show and audience were enough to overlook the slight.

Northern Ireland

Another of my most memorable broadcasts occurred during my tenure at WNWS. The situation in Northern Ireland was tense. People were bombing each other. The endless conflict between Catholics and Protestants made little sense to most Americans.

One Saturday night, I made a phone call to Maze Prison in Northern Ireland. Bobby Sands, a Catholic and IRA member, was fifty to sixty days into his hunger strike. He was imprisoned for his participation in criminals acts by the IRA. Many say that Sands was wrongly accused, and today he has become a martyr.

Sands was trying to show the existence of oppression against Catholics by the ruling Protestants with the support of the British government. While in prison, Sands was elected to Parliament. But his health had deteriorated at the time we called Maze Prison. Sands so strongly believed in his cause that he was willing to commit suicide through starving himself to death to gain attention for the plight of his countrymen. People had called in to the show say how inhumane the conditions were at the prison. So I called the prison to talk with the person in charge—or just talk with anybody I could.

One of the things the listeners had said is that there was no toilet paper in the cells. The prison manager I talked with said, of course, there was toilet paper. I didn't know if it was true, and toilet paper wasn't the issue. The interest was to give the people direct access and perhaps involvement in an international event. It sure made for great talk radio.

I was funneled to a guard near Bobby Sands cell. It turned out that Bobby's mother was there. She was pleading with her son to get him to eat. The guard refused our request, but he did give us his perspective on the situation. He said the conflict was about poor people and poorer people who felt powerless themselves. Sands died in prison less than a week later. There were no winners, only losers. Again, it was riveting radio.

In the end though there was little the local listening public could do because this incident related to something happening several thousand miles and an ocean away. American citizens didn't believe this was a situation to seek US intervention.

The following week, there was a memo sent by Lou Krone, the GM, stating that we needed prior approval for all long-distance calls. He summoned me to his office and screamed, "What are you doing?" I replied it was a great interview. He still didn't want me to make the calls, regardless of programming quality.

Stepping on Toes

Not long after that, Neil Rogers, the talk host, took on the additional role of program director. Rogers had attacked Governor Bob Graham. He called him Graham Crackers. He made fun of him. But when Graham came on his program, Rogers treated him like pablum. Everyone at the station felt that Rogers was being incredibly hypocritical. As a result, there was a feeling that Rogers didn't do his job with any degree of credibility.

Above all else, most of us working in talk radio respect the medium as a vehicle for the public. To be hypocritical like Rogers was to betray a public trust. So I went on the air that Saturday night and told Dennis Sanders, the board operator, that I was going to talk about Neil's interview with the governor. Nobody else at the station was willing to discuss it publicly. We both knew it could be a problem, but our credibility as a legitimate news source was at issue.

I talked about the blandness Rogers exhibited to Graham in person but nastiness when the governor wasn't around. About ten minutes later, Rogers walked into the station and sat behind the glass between the studio and the control room. I took a break, and Rogers walked into the studio and said, "That's it. It's over. You're done."

I wasn't sure what to do. Should I stay and fight for the show or leave? I decided it was best to leave. They got a ton of calls at the station condemning Rogers because I legitimately criticized Rogers for his handling of the interview with the governor.

On the way home, I was listening to Larry Kent (now deceased) on WINZ.

He got a call that said, "Larry, you should hear what just happened at your competition. Neil Rogers just took Mike Siegel off the air."

Then out of the blue came Kent's on-air response, "Mike Siegel, if you're listening. You have an open mike right here."

I wanted to go, but I felt it would be unprofessional and inappropriate before talking to the GM of WNWS. It was pointless to pursue anything there because of Neil's stature. A week later, I went on Larry Kent's show at the competing station and told what happened. I haven't hosted a radio show based in Miami since. Sadly, Neil Rogers passed away on December 24, 2010 at the age of 68.

Radio belongs to the public. The public demands and deserves the truth.

CHASING THE LIGHTS

Where they make a desert, they call it peace.

—Cornelius Tacitus, ca. 98

"You die. That's your problem."

In July 1981, while I was working at WNWS in Miami, I had the opportunity to travel to Israel with thirteen other journalists. Fighting was occurring in the Middle East, but it wasn't as intense as it had been only a few years before. So it seemed relatively safe to go, and I would do the public a great service by reporting from another part of the world. Besides, there was a strong Jewish listenership in Florida that would be very interested in getting direct information from that region.

My job was to call in reports from Metullah, a little kibbutz on the northern border of Israel about three miles across from Lebanon. The station thought I was going to be discussing the Middle East from a cultural and local viewpoint. In fact, that's what I intended.

We were housed in a modest hotel in Metullah and had reasonably free run of the town. But our hosts were nervous about us staying because of Palestine Liberation Organization attacks. The fear of any information getting to the Palestinians was tremendous. The uneasiness of our hosts became clear when they said that if the PLO knew there were some Jewish American journalists so close to the border, we would be target practice.

I'm not sure what happened soon thereafter, but something caused us to be told we would have to leave. Our Israeli hosts were trying to protect us but were also quite effectively keeping us from doing our jobs. After all, we were journalists, and I wanted to aggressively report back to America what was really happening in the Middle East.

I talked with my fellow reporters, but they didn't seem interested in pursuing anything further. I wouldn't let it lie though, and I put together a petition asking for the right to stay. Northern Israel was of great interest to all of our readers and listeners. I wanted to find out what was happening and report it for my listeners. That meant I was going to have to use talk-radio skills in convincing the others to stay with me.

The quest for truth came out in all the journalists, and I was pleased when we all signed the petition. I marched into the Israeli government's press office and evoked every bit of righteous indignation I could in my best Yiddish. The press officer, Rafi Horowitz, seemed a bit perturbed about even having to handle such a chore, but after further persuading, the petition was taken to the chief of staff of the Israeli army. This was Lieutenant General Rafael Eitan, who showed his leadership by quickly making a decision.

I heard one loud voice coming from the other room, and Horowitz scurried out. I remember the very simple words directed to me.

"The general said," relayed the press officer, "you want to stay at the hotel? Okay."

I was elated!

"You get in my way, that's my problem. You die, that's your problem. We have plenty of people experienced in writing obituaries."

That last statement cut into my elation just a bit.

I thought he was being a bit melodramatic. After all, we were being protected by one of the most efficient fighting forces on earth. I excitedly ran off to tell the others we were going to get our story.

By the time we all got back to the hotel, there was an Israeli Defense Force agent waiting to brief us about conditions.

He said, "Don't congregate in groups. You will be a target. Don't wear helmets. You will be a target. Don't use electronic equipment in the open. You will be a target."

By this time I was getting nervous myself and was glad to hear that there was a bomb shelter up the street. We were told that attacks often come in the night. They were strafing attacks, almost like snipers. You couldn't see them ahead of time. You could only hear the whistling of the armament. I'm sure it was right about that time that I questioned my own sanity for even being there.

The defense force agent then added that in the event of an attack at night, the hotel we were staying in was a target. We shouldn't even try to get to the bomb shelter.

"Just get to the basement as fast as you can. Don't worry about your papers or your clothes. Get to the basement," he said very deliberately.

My room was on the hotel top floor. Before the darkness fell, I got a call through to my parents to say good-byes just in case.

The excitement of the trip had prevented me from sleeping for thirty-six hours, but I was exhausted. After the call to my parents, I fell asleep. About two in the morning, there was a gigantic thunder and lightning storm. The night sky seemed almost like day because of the flashes of light from above. Then I noticed that this was like no thunder or lightning I had ever seen or heard. My grogginess immediately went away, and I distinctly remember the hairs on my neck standing with fear.

This was no storm. We were under attack. It was continuous. I foolishly poked my head out the window, and there were screams from the wounded shadows running in the blackness lit by the bombs. It was a wonder we hadn't already been hit. The bombs were right over our heads and landing all around us. It was only a matter of time before my room became rubble.

I literally jumped out through my hotel room door and began knocking on doors. I've never been so frantic in my life. I was shouting, "Get to the basement! Get to the basement!" My friends and others staying in the hotel came running out in bathrobes, shorts, yesterday's shirts—whatever.

The elevators, such as they were, had already been disabled. We scrambled down the back staircase, thinking that was somehow more secure. It's amazing how fast the human body can move when the adrenaline is pumping out of fear.

Later, after we were safe below the earth, someone pointed out to me how cute I looked in my underwear. I had forgotten to put any pants on in my rush to get everybody up. As we were congratulating ourselves on making it safely to the basement, we realized that we were missing two people. One was a Catholic priest who hosted a radio show, and another was a Daytona Beach newscaster. Maurice Lewis, a friend of mine who was a Boston anchorman, looked at me, and we bolted back upstairs to get our two absentees.

As we ran up the stairs, we could feel the shaking of the building from the explosions. All of a sudden, in my mind I envisioned the mammoth concrete structure that housed us exploding like a balloon.

Maurice and I were pounding on every door, yelling at the top of our lungs. We finally found them both, who turned out to be the heaviest sleepers I have ever known. In fact, they were complaining about all the noise we were making. They both thought we were partying the night away. You should have seen the look on their faces when they realized what was happening.

Looking back now, it's almost comical. At the time though, it was terrifying.

There was an ABC News camera crew there with us. Unfortunately, their on-air personality was safely tucked away in Jerusalem. The crew complained about having to be there in harm's way only to shoot the scene and make it appear like the on-air talent was in the middle of everything. I learned a little bit that night about TV that I had never realized.

The morning finally came, and the bombing had stopped. The swimming pool at the hotel had been destroyed. I don't know how many lives were lost. Those figures were closely guarded by the Israeli government. They never wanted the PLO to know they had found any level of success.

The PLO weapons that night were Soviet-made Katyusha rockets. They weren't very accurate at all. Their margin of error was 1.5 miles, a far cry from sophisticated guided bombs used in the Gulf War less than ten years later. To the Israelis, the Palestinians didn't care about targets or accuracy. To the Israelis near the Lebanon border, they were all at risk, whether they were in a tank or a temple.

We climbed to the roof of the hotel, and we could see a caravan of the Israeli Defense Force marching from Israel to Lebanon. There were tanks and artillery vehicles. There were things moving along and being carried that must have been military weaponry, but I had no idea what kind it was. And there was artillery—lots and lots of artillery.

To give the train of armaments cover for the ground troops, we saw the daylight sky become almost black with F-16 fighters. These fighters were slowly moving along, protecting the troops, and waiting for the right moment when ground artillery and the jets could coordinate the onslaught.

The target was Beaufort Castle, completed in AD 1139. It had become a PLO hideout in the mountains just across the Israeli-Lebanese southern border overlooking the Litani River valley. You could see the smoke from the bombs the jets had just dropped into the hills. The natural beauty of the area had long since faded, scarred by bombs and bodies.

You could almost feel the heat on the rockets shot from Israeli ground. But nothing seemed to do much damage. The castle was surrounded by the ring of mountains. Perhaps the Israeli plan was to strip away the trees with explosions to expose the enemy fortress. Or maybe the plan was just to violently defend their homeland with counterattacks. Regardless, this war was destroying lives, lands, and futures.

I had never been a war correspondent, never really wanted to be one. Now, I knew I didn't want to be one. Leave it to the Edward R. Murrows and Ernie Pyles of the world.

We weren't allowed to stay any longer because it was clear that a very intense battle was about to take place. I didn't argue, and there certainly wasn't any righteous indignation.

It was amazing to see how the people who lived in kibbutzim existed. Every night was fear. Even on those nights where nothing happened, it would seem that the silence would only bring terror.

I don't know how anyone could sleep through the night. It's funny, the word *sleep* wasn't used. Sleep was something in the past. It had become little more than a few minutes' nap. The ever constant state of fear from the Soviet near-random rockets was what led Israeli prime minister Menachem Begin to adopt the campaign slogan, "No more Katyusha rockets in Northern Israel."

Lights, Camera, Action in Palm Beach

When I returned from Israel, I settled back into the explosive issue concerning local measured telephone service that I discussed in the previous chapter. The exposure I received from the reports on the Israeli-Lebanese border caused a rise in my popularity, and I became a TV host as well. My show was *Good Morning, Palm Beaches* and was on live at six thirty and nine thirty mornings on WPEC TV, the ABC affiliate. The show had a cohost, Anne Forsythe, and wrapped around *Good Morning America*.

This was television and not nearly as hard-hitting as the radio program. It was close to the infotainment of today's news. I really wasn't comfortable with my role because of the restraint I had to use in questions and topics. The station demographics were middle- and upper-income people who generally don't rock the boat. In fact, many of those people made money from the very system that my listeners on radio shows often question.

The show had some appeal but gave me a grueling schedule. It was almost like being back in New Hampshire. I got up at 4:00 a.m. to go to the television station. After the second live show ended at 10:00 a.m., I would do postproduction work until about 11:00 a.m. Then I would go home for a few hours of sleep before doing the 6:00–8:00 p.m. radio show in Miami.

We did some provocative work on the show. This was in the early 1980s, and to give a voice on television to M. T. Mehdi, the chairman of the American-Arab Relations Committee, was a bit unusual. Even more off the beaten track was the interview with Father Phil Scheiding, a gay Catholic priest. Too often though the show consisted of interviews with clothing designers or health-club managers. It just wasn't what I wanted to do.

During this time a few of the city fathers decided that it was a privilege to live in Palm Beach. I agree. It was. But these council members wanted to build a wall around the city through the use of a Palm Beach identification card. The proposal stated that in order to cross the bridge into Palm Beach, you were going to have to carry your special ID.

When I heard that, I thought I was living in either a totalitarian society or a science-fiction movie. I'm not sure I've ever been more animated about an issue than I was about the Palm Beach ID card. Nonresidents were going to be able to get a work visa, and residents would have special privileges.

This proposal was the first strike in class warfare that would keep certain extremely wealthy residents—many of whom were part-time residents—from seeing anyone else. Regardless of the fact that Palm Beach received federal and state tax revenue, a few elitists believed they could keep other taxpayers out.

My gosh! This was an attempt to restrict travel inside the United States! If this had gone further, there most certainly would have been constitutional arguments about this ordinance.

It was even more interesting that the origin of this proposal was ambiguous. Nobody seemed to claim credit for it, and the Palm Beach ID card had been surreptitiously discussed behind council's closed doors. Isn't government in America supposed to be out in the open, available to the public for participation? We exposed this horrendous usurpation of freedom on *Good Morning, Palm Beaches*. The local public was outraged. There was an embarrassment and a quick retreat. The proposal never came up again.

The television show ended live production soon thereafter. Live television is expensive, and the schedule was too much for me anyway. For whatever reason, I was totally without a position in broadcasting for the first time in many years.

It was time for me to contemplate my future.

TRANSITIONS

Our government rests in public opinion.
Whoever can change public opinion can change
the government practically just so much.

—Abraham Lincoln, 1856

Broadcasting, Law, Politics

The loss of the radio show in Miami and ending live production of the television show caused me to determine whether I wanted to go forward with the career of talk-show host.

I was single with no children. But the moving among stations was starting to wear on me. I already had my doctorate in communications and quite a lot of experience from which to teach. Yet the issues of the day, the thrill of debate, and public service was like a rabbit in front of me. And I was the greyhound out in front.

In 1982 I enrolled in law school in southern Florida and found the study exhilarating. At the same time I worked part-time at several stations over the next three years. Law school was a means to an end, or so I thought, and talk radio provided me the income to keep food on my table. Essentially, I was like most of the students working part-time to support themselves. For the first time in years, I blended in with the crowd.

The time I spent in law school gave me the opportunity to think about the future. I had always wanted to make a difference in this world—to help improve the quality of human life. I was having doubts about being able to do that through the medium I had worked in for so many years.

The campaigns we ran on radio gave voices to people who believed they were powerless. Talk radio gave them a collective strength and a place where they would be heard. Many of the shows I did related to charitable causes. I was always proud to be able to show to the world those people who were providing selfless service to others. The shows I've talked about helped many people and some to even reach their dreams.

At the same time, the people in Palm Beach didn't need any help with a public voice. I loved the area, but many of the local officials and community leaders were a group of people who knew the system well. They knew how to manipulate government. In fact, some of them were the very ones who were causing many of the problems of the bought-and-paid-for government.

But I did find a healthy respect, even from those whom I criticized. One of my warmest moments on radio was the day I was admitted to the bar. The listeners at the Palm Beach station where I was a part-time host organized a congratulatory ceremony. Or maybe they were hoping I would leave the air. I always wondered about that.

I actually lived in Sunrise, a small town about 50 miles from Palm Beach. I hadn't been paying much attention to city politics because I had all I could handle with law school and making a living. Not long after I was admitted to the bar, a special election was being held in Sunrise for mayor. The past mayor, John Lomelo, had been indicted for improprieties and had to leave office. He was later convicted in federal court.

A Broward County commissioner called me at the station and asked to meet for lunch the next day. He said there was something he wanted to talk about. I agreed to meet him but was prepared to get an earful because I had been particularly critical of some area officials.

I was very surprised at the topic. He wanted me to run for mayor of Sunrise.

The commissioner said, "Mike, I wouldn't want to face you in a debate. But there's a lot more to winning an election than just debating. You have to get out among the people."

Unfortunately, I had little time to consider it because the filing deadline was less than a week away, and the election would take place in only seven weeks. I'm not one to waste time in making decisions, and I weighed the pluses and minuses of being in office. For several years, I had been criticizing government officials for being responsive only to special interests. I believed I could do better, and a career in public service would enable me to use my education and communication skills. Also, I would have a chance to build a better world.

I decided to run and set out to reach the people with my messages. There was no way I had the time to raise the money needed for a media campaign. In order to reach the voters with my plans for tackling the local problems, I had to knock on doors.

This was brutal. It was August in southern Florida, and I knocked on doors every day and evening for six straight weeks. I spent about half of that time on one condominium complex with eight thousand units!

It got to the point where I felt I had this masochistic drive to see how much of the heat I could take, but it was a tremendous experience. There were three people in the race. One was the current city council president, and the other was an aide to the indicted mayor. Both had high name recognition and many years of involvement in the community.

Then there was me. I didn't know anything about the nuances of campaigning, and I'm not sure yet who was supporting me and who was for my opponents. Ultimately, I came in second, and was proud of my finish.

After the election, I started practicing law in Sunrise and doing part-time radio. At the same time, I traveled several times to Boston to see friends. One friend was an executive in a mortgage company, and she said that if I were in Boston, I could do the closings for the company.

Cooler Weather

It was hard to leave Florida, but there's an appeal of Boston that anyone with a law degree would feel. I moved to Boston and hung out my shingle at the Faneuil Hall Office Building. This stately old structure had been the site of many prerevolution speeches. You could sense the men with their muskets on the lookout for red coats listening to orators speak of freedom. It was awe-inspiring, the kind of place that makes you proud of our nation's heritage and of the great courage it must have taken to combat the forces of King George.

Ironically, the people who owned the station where I was a host in Palm Beach also owned a station in Framingham, Massachusetts, a city just outside Boston. I started doing a daily two-hour talk show focused on the issues of the day.

This seemed like a dream life. I lived in a condominium overlooking Boston Commons, practiced law, and was on radio. I enjoyed this life for a full year.

In mid-1987 I got a call from Rick Sklar, who was then considered one of the great people in radio. In fact, he created the Top 40 format at WABC in New York in the 1950s. He was a consultant at the time for WMCA in New York and asked me to do fill-in for Barry Gray and Barry Farber. Gray was one of the first talk hosts in the nation. He was a DJ playing music in the 1940s and then started taking phone calls about various topics. But the technology wasn't interactive; they couldn't take phone calls while on the air. So Gray would repeat the question or comment and then talk about the issue.

Both Gray and Farber were still at WMCA. They had over sixty years of radio experience between them, and to even be asked to do fill-in work for these icons of the siedustry was an honor. I jumped at the chance and commuted between Boston and New York for my occasional fill-in work. It was hectic, but it was soon apparent to me that practicing law was not what I wanted to do. My passion is now and was then for talk radio and all that it allows me to accomplish.

Frank Oxarart was the GM at WMCA. He liked my worked and offered me a full-time afternoon program.

Wow! My own show in New York, the number one market in the nation, and my boyhood stomping grounds! Once again, I had to give a quick answer.

On the way back to LaGuardia, I thought about my first years in radio and how exciting it was. I considered the ups and downs from New Hampshire to Florida. I could sense the feeling of the Boston Commons and the history that seeps through anytime you hear the bells that Paul Revere once heard. But talk radio was at my core.

As I settled into my seat on the plane back home, I knew what I wanted to do. So why wait? I reached to the back of the seat in front of me, unhooked the satellite phone, and called WMCA.

"Frank, I like your offer. If you cover my airfare between Boston and New York for a month to give me time to relocate, it's a deal," I said.

"Then welcome back to New York, Mike. It's a deal!" was his response.

Even the commute for that month wasn't bad. It took me twenty minutes to get to the airport in Boston, another forty-five minutes to fly to New York, and then another thirty minutes to WMCA. There are many people in cities around the country that have a longer commute.

During that month I made a final commitment to talk radio. My legal education was a tremendous advantage. It helped me in so many ways. But practicing law wasn't what I wanted to do. After a month I moved to Midtown Manhattan on the forty-first floor of a forty-two-story building. The station was only a five-minute walk away.

Over the next year I handled so many issues of local and national prominence that I just can't remember all of them. It really was a blur. But then, as I was feeling very comfortable and gaining a foothold in New York, WMCA was sold to a Christian broadcast group. I knew the reputation of the new owners, and they were good at what they did. The format change was not going to include what I had to offer.

So the job I wanted to last forever evaporated. I didn't want to leave New York, but I was willing to travel to do fill-ins. One station who called was KING radio in Seattle. The new program director was Brian Jennings, and in October 1988 the station flew me across country for a three-day interview. This was a lot of effort just for fill-in work, but it didn't make much sense for the station or for me to fly six thousand miles round-trip and not have a complete examination of what I could do.

My three days ended, and by the time I had landed back in New York, KING had offered me a full-time position.

It wasn't what I was looking for. Seattle was a beautiful city, but I had only been in New York for a year. I called some of my friends and people I respected in radio around the country about the offer. They said that Seattle was the kind of city that could use some fresh broadcast energy and that a good talk-radio station there was sorely needed. Plus, my mother and father had very happy memories of their brief time in the Pacific Northwest as newlyweds and were supportive of the move.

My family and friends said, "Go for it!"

So I did.

THUGS AND DRUGS
IN EMERALD CITY

The administration of justice lies at
the foundation of government.

—William Howard Taft, 1908

Understanding Seattle

In November 15, 1988, I started full time at KING radio in Seattle. The station was owned by the Bullitt family. They were well connected, charitable, and liberal minded. They were and are pillars of the Puget Sound.

Before I went on the air, I spent a week talking with people in the city about the community issues. One of the persons I met with was Seattle council member Norm Rice. We talked for several hours. It was a great conversation, and I felt comfortable with Seattle from Rice and from Cary Bozeman, the executive director of the Boys and Girls Club, and several local reporters, including Jean Enerson, a popular TV news anchor.

I also talked with people on the street, just asking questions and listening. I read newspaper clippings about local government officials and couldn't help but notice that there was a significant hands-off approach in the area from the media about local public people. This made no sense to me. I dug a little further, called a few elected officials, and found a basic mediocrity in area government. There was no rampant corruption. There wasn't the quality of people in the state legislature or in local governments who would provide leadership to the area. It was abundantly and unfortunately clear that leadership and innovation in my new home came from the private sector—not from government.

On November 21, I went on the air. Tim Hill, King County executive, seemed to do little more than occupy space. Governor Booth Gardner was an administrator but hardly a leader. The term "Go along to get along" must have been invented in Washington State's government.

The response I received at first was not particularly positive. It seemed almost heresy to criticize people in elected or appointed positions.

"We don't say bad things about people here," was the phrase I was told several times in my first week.

My response was invariably, "Isn't the job of talk radio to provoke discussion? And if one is going to ask for the public trust while serving in government, then isn't it reasonable to be accountable for your actions?"

"That sounds like New York," was a retort to me.

I began to feel that I had made a mistake.

I had the support of KING General Manager Bob Golucci though, who said he wanted more coverage of gang activity in Seattle. This was a problem "swept under the rug," he said. "It needs to be brought into the open."

One of the things we learned at KING radio came in an internal memo from chief of police Patrick Fitzsimons. The memo was sent to lower-ranking police officials and indicated that the department shouldn't talk about gangs in Seattle. Moreover, the phrase "gang problem" wouldn't be used. The reason was that Fitzsimons and other city officials didn't want anyone to know there was such a problem in the Emerald City.

This veil of secrecy around a problem which could affect thousands of residents had been tried in Portland. It didn't work there, and it wasn't going to work in Seattle.

This was a major miscalculation by Fitzsimons, especially because there was indeed a gang problem in Seattle. The diversity of population, poverty, and educational differences all contributed to the flourishing of gangs in my new home. Gangs from southern California, the Bloods and the Crips, found a new city to easily infiltrate. In fact, I even talked with two gang members from out of state who said that Seattle was "Ours to be had," and they intended to take it. What the gangs brought with them were violence and drugs.

The problem eventually became enormous, and it took too much time and energy to find anyone to speak on the record about gangs because the police chief and city officials would not acknowledge the problem. It was like a heroin abuser refusing to admit the addiction.

I believe the proliferation of gangs was clearly the responsibility of police chief Patrick Fitzsimons. He wouldn't confront the problem and wouldn't engage the community in helping to at least identify gang thugs.

From my experience in Newark as a teacher and in other cities working on difficult issues, it's clear that criminals don't want to be exposed. Sure, gangs want to be feared, but they don't want to be identified. The Seattle Police Department's policy of secrecy prevented the line officers and the public from possessing an important weapon against thugs—exposure.

The gangs added to an already-growing drug problem in Seattle. FBI reports acknowledged that a large amount of the nation's drugs came through the Pacific Northwest either through the ports of Seattle or nearby Vancouver, British Columbia. Some of the horror of drug abuse was bound to roost in Seattle.

I befriended former police sergeant, Chuck Pillon, who had been involved in a major controversy while at the department. Pillon was very aggressive in shutting down crack houses. Pillon said that

Fitzsimons didn't want that kind of strong police work. No criminal defendant claimed Pillon violated his constitutional rights, but Fitzsimons tried to stop Pillon's aggressive approach to stopping the drug trade in Seattle. Pillon was taken off the street and offered a desk job. He refused. He believed his work was out in the field.

Again, this didn't make sense to me because it was clear that Seattle had a substantial drug problem, and gangs were on the rise. So why not get aggressive in stopping crime and earning the reputation that gang violence would not be tolerated in this beautiful, pristine city?

So I looked into Fitzsimons's background in New York, where he had been a police officer. I tried to understand him better. What I found was that Fitzsimons had a certain philosophy coming out of New York's Knapp Commission. This was the group that studied and found pervasive corruption in New York's police.

In my investigation, I was told that Fitzsimons was instructed to handle drugs in this way:

1. Don't do anything aggressively with crack houses because you may wind up in a situation of possible corruption. If police go into a crack house and find a lot of cash there and if the cash goes missing, there's an immediate possibility that the police put the money in their pockets. There is always the cloud of corruption.
2. When you're aggressive, there's the possibility of police being involved in activities that are inappropriate. Avoid even the temptation of scandal at all costs.

Essentially, Fitzsimons worked in New York under the theory of avoiding lawsuits rather than deterring crime.

It seemed to me that this philosophy was the same as saying that all police officers were capable of being corrupted, that they were all dishonest people. No community can prosper under that type of paranoia.

Police scandals made the mayor and city council look bad. So when Fitzsimons brought his lawsuit-avoidance philosophy to

Seattle, it pleased city leaders. Apparently these leaders wanted a passive police presence, and they got it with Fitzsimons.

I talked about all of this on the air and found a festering sore inside the Seattle Police Department. Several of the rank-and-file officers were extremely encouraging because they felt their hands were being tied. I talked with officers who told me they weren't being given the freedom to do their jobs.

In fact, one officer called me on the air saying, "Give us one week of freedom to do our jobs within the constitution, and we'll clean up the city."

The policy of the Seattle Police Department was to not clash with certain minority groups even if they were criminals. The strong inference was that the police policy was to place a proverbial fence around areas where gang members lived and contain violence and drug trade to those areas.

At the same time, leaders of the affected minority communities were calling the station off the air and asking for help. They wanted the police to come in and weren't getting a satisfactory response. The minority community leaders wanted their neighborhoods to be treated like nonminorities. That meant getting gangs and drugs off their streets.

Needless to say, this didn't bode well for me in terms of developing a working relationship with the mayor and the police chief. It was an unwillingness, not an inability, on the part of the Seattle Police Department and the mayor's office to stop the crime problem in Seattle.

That demonstrates the power of and opportunities created through talk radio. I have always believed that the main purpose of talk radio was to be a provocateur, an avenue for people to discuss what is wrong and offer solutions to fix the problems. Sure, we could talk about good things and what is right, but I think it's essential to also discuss and offer solutions to improve our society.

Some among Seattle's elite didn't like it that problems, swept under the rug for years, were now becoming public. I soon found out that my show was a topic of conversation at cocktail soirees downtown. Word got back to me that the elite wanted Mike Siegel to "shut up."

One night, an investigative reporter with KING radio, Jeff Ray, and I were traveling the city with Chuck Pillon. Chuck was a private investigator by that time. Frank LaChance from Neighbors Against Drugs joined us. We chose to go into a dark area of the city. It was known to be a drug haven.

One thug came hurriedly up to us and offered to sell us crack. Pillon paid $10 for a vial. We went down the street, gave it to a police officer, and gave a description of the crack seller. There was an article in the paper the next day that the police had arrested the drug dealer.

That night confirmed my reputation at KING for being aggressive. But again, my aggressiveness didn't make me popular with many people in Seattle's city hall. I had to dig for information without cooperation or even responses from city officials. But many lower in the municipal government food chain talked willingly on condition of anonymity.

On other occasions we would follow police officers—with permission—into areas where there was thought to be gang and drug activity. I doubted that Fitzsimons knew the officers were permitting it, but after witnessing drug crimes on almost every late-night trip, it was obvious we were being tipped off by the police on the beats. The officers really wanted our support. They told me time after time how much they appreciated the opportunity for the public to know firsthand how it happened on the street.

More and more police talked to us, again on condition of anonymity, about the lack of leadership within the Seattle Police Department. We were able to communicate a lot of good information to the public as a result of the cooperation we received from the rank and file. We also regularly received SPD internal memos from our sources inside the department showing the lack of will to aggressively attack the drug and gang problems of the city.

I've never understood the reluctance of the city officials to aggressively attack the illegal drug trade. Substances and abusers cause untold damage in families and communities long after the abusers themselves have died from their toxicity they placed in their own bodies. It was especially harmful in minority neighborhoods. Our nation's recent history has shown too much indifference, which some believe is almost encouragement, of drugs in minority areas. It is certainly not a compassionate view of humanity to favor enforcement for some but not all.

The general public told me they benefited from the discussions on gangs and drugs in the Seattle area. But I soon learned this was not a problem that would go away anytime in the near future.

The difficulties and conflicts with law enforcement issues would continue for several years thereafter and would follow me wherever I went around the Puget Sound. I wouldn't relent on the need for public involvement, for disclosure, and for responsibility. None of those seemed to interest the person who became Seattle's mayor.

A FIFTY-ONE PERCENT CONGRESSIONAL PAY RAISE?

The passion for office among members
of Congress is very great, if not absolutely
disreputable, and greatly embarasses
the operations of government.

—James K. Polk, 1846

"We need another Boston Tea Party."

Roy Fox and his wife, Mary, and I were friends from talk-show-host conventions. We were aware of each other's work, and they had commented about my activist radio success.

Roy had a radio talk show on WXYT in Detroit. In December 1988 I received a call from Mary, who abruptly declared, "Mike. It's time for a national protest."

"I don't understand," I replied.

It seems that a fellow called into her husband's show and said, "Look, I'm a struggling small businessman in the Detroit area. I pay my bills and help my employees whenever I can. I have to shell out of my pocket more each day to comply with continual increases in regulations coming from everywhere, and then I pay more in taxes for what I don't need! We need another Boston Tea Party or something. I just can't sit by and stand for taxation without representation."

Mary told me she had never heard someone so adamant about an issue. What the caller was talking about was that Congress was about to sneak themselves a raise. Then she said something about "politicians soaking the public," and it got my attention.

In 1988, a little known nonpartisan committee called the Quadrennial Commission was empowered to consider the salaries of Congress. The Commission was headed up by Lloyd Cutler, the consummate Washington–DC beltway lobbyist. For years he had handled various lobbying efforts and had been doling out campaign cash to candidates who would become members of Congress. Now, he was being lobbied by Congress for a raise.

This raise wasn't just a cost-of-living increase. Cutler's group found that a whopping 51 percent pay hike for Congress was in order!

I was glad that Mary had called because this was a perfect springboard for a national initiative.

Roy handled Detroit and parts of the East Coast, I worked in Seattle and the West Coast, and a national campaign was soon coordinated. Talk-show hosts from around the country reported that their listeners have loudly spoken: a 51 percent pay increase for Congress would be outrageous!

But it wasn't going to be enough to just speak or even write letters. We needed something more demonstrative. Going back into history and following up on the idea first stated by the Detroit small-business owner, we decided to start the Tea Bag Campaign.

This Tea Bag Campaign enabled Americans to participate in a way that wouldn't be too costly and would be a loud but peaceful "action speaking louder than words." The reference in history would be patriotic and remind Congress of the importance of the first tea party in the American colonies. Like the action on the Boston Harbor before the Revolutionary War, the people were showing they were ready to engage an aloof leadership in a battle.

During the Tea Bag Campaign, I was on the air as the coordinator of all the radio stations around the country. I gave regular updates of progress, responses from Congress, and reported what listeners from around the country were saying.

Interestingly enough, nobody from the Quadrennial Commission would ever come on the air with me to discuss their recommendation to increase congressional salaries by 51 percent. My staff called. I called. But despite their being appointed to serve and paid by the citizens, the commissioners were unwilling to speak in public.

I would give out information about who to call or write and encourage people to make their views known. Members of Congress were being inundated. Their phone lines were full. Their fax machines were running out of paper. This was the first nationally coordinated campaign that I know of where local talk-radio stations played such a big role.

The message was loud and clear to Congress, "No pay raise!"

Talk show stations in nearly every state participated in the Tea Bag Campaign. Ralph Nader from Public Citizen and David Keating from the National Taxpayers Union got involved. They agreed to collect the tea bags and were elated that nearly one hundred thousand tea bags were sent for delivery to the doorstep of congress.

Yet that wasn't enough. We knew at KING that we were an integral part of something historic. This may have been the most dramatic grassroots uprising since the nation was formed, and it was important to make sure the people had a voice. Their elected representatives sure weren't going to do it. They were running from this issue like sprinters at the Olympics.

I vowed I would stay inside the KING building until we got one million tea bags sent to Washington, DC. I wanted there to be no doubt in the minds of Congress that the public was united in their stand against the pay raise. Local and national press were all over the story. This wasn't a publicity stunt for publicity's sake. This got the issue covered.

After two weeks, the tea bags were mounting in DC. I was prepared to help get those one million tea bags until Ralph Nader called. He said what was happening was great. Congress was feeling the pressure. Then he asked, "Can you come to the Hill to testify?"

I didn't want to break my promise. We hadn't reached the million-tea-bag count yet. But we were looking for the result of no pay raise. Across the country the national momentum was peaking. This totally American movement seemed to be working. Now, I was being asked to be a spokesperson for those who couldn't go to Congress themselves. The right thing to do was end the stay inside KING and talk for the public at congress.

The listeners on KING were unanimous in their support for me going. This was important because I had made a commitment to collect the one million tea bags. The people desperately needed someone in public life to keep their commitments to them. So I felt I had to get permission from the listeners before going.

Testifying before Congress was quite humbling. Even a congressional subcommittee is awe-inspiring when the power of our federal government is being considered. The chairman of the Senate Government Operations Committee was Senator John Glenn of Ohio. He was a hero to many—including me. As an astronaut, he saw the globe from a perspective very few have ever seen.

I admit now to being somewhat apprehensive about making the appearance. Neither international television nor national radio ever made me as nervous as I was that day before the United States Senate.

Senator Glenn looked at me, wrinkled his eye, and bellowed, "You're the guy who sent me a lifetime supply of tea bags."

It broke the ice and sent me a message that the people had been heard. I then felt we had the upper hand. The humor of the moment assured me at the very least we would get a fair hearing.

I began my testimony by telling the committee about the businessman from Detroit. Then I discussed what the callers were saying. Few questions came to me from the senators, but it wouldn't have mattered. I still remember today feeling the pride well up inside me from the public charge I had been given by people throughout America. This wasn't Mike Siegel at that committee as much as it was Jane from Seattle, John from Chicago, Sam from New York, or Sarah from Dallas. It was the United States of America who was speaking, and I was honored to be her mouthpiece.

At the end of my testimony there was applause from the audience and a polite thank-you from the senate. And Senator Glenn did kindly invite me to tea at his office. "Anytime for the next fifty years!" he said as he chuckled.

I spent that week doing my program at KING in Seattle from our nation's capitol. The intensity of the situation mounted. Regardless of the immense public pressure, Congress was isolated within the boundaries of the Hill.

I went on the air with stations around the country and told them minute by minute which member of Congress had decided and who was as of yet uncommitted. It was the uncommitted member of Congress who became our focus. At one point, I got the fax number for then Speaker of the House Jim Wright of Texas. It was on a Friday, and I went on the air with a considerable number of stations. I rattled off the fax number time after time. By Monday morning, there was paper all over the floor in the speaker's office. The fax paper had been used up, and the machine's red light was blinking, "Add paper, add paper." I heard later that every fax message told the speaker to vote *no* to the pay raise.

Wright was neither pleased nor amused. He immediately had the fax number changed to a private number. Imagine that! A member of Congress with a private fax number! You would think he didn't want to hear from the people!

We would have people call Senator Glenn's office. I was on the air in Cleveland—Glenn's state—with WERE radio and made the point that Ohio citizens should be contacting the senator. He got many calls from his own constituents in Ohio. That was much of what we did in that campaign—encouraging people to call their own elected members of Congress.

The final straw for the Congress was when they took a brief break. Democratic members went on a retreat in West Virginia to a very posh private resort. They took their families every year. It was something of a pause to repose and reflect for the Democrats. We found the phone number of the resort and gave it out on the air on a

Friday. For that entire weekend, the phones were blown off the hook at the resort; the members couldn't even find peace despite the fact they had gone there for a retreat.

It got the point across. After the break, Congress came back into session and chose to stop the pay raise.

The way they had to do that, by the way, was that the Quadrennial Commission had to make the 51 percent increase proposal, and then President Reagan had to approve it to take it to the floor of Congress for a vote. If Congress did nothing, it automatically went into effect as a pay raise. In spite of all the public pressure, members of Congress didn't want to vote on it. They wanted the raise. Privately they were telling Speaker Wright to "Hold tough. Don't let the vote happen!"

In and of itself, the fact that members of Congress would define a "tough" position as one which enabled them to postpone a vote was absurd. It showed a lack of spine on the part of Congress. At the very least, if they're going to hold office, they should be willing to stand up for their convictions.

The people's campaign to stop the congressional pay hike became so widespread and powerful that Congress was forced to take a vote. If no vote had been taken, there would have been incumbents turned out in droves at the next election.

Overwhelmingly, in the House and Senate, Congress rejected the pay raise. You should have heard the speeches of patriotism and duty and love for country in the remarks on the floor about how the pay raise was the wrong thing to do. What took minutes for the public to determine took months for Congress to realize.

KING Program Director Brian Jennings forwarded a call to me from a listener after we won that vote. He offered to buy us drinks at any bar in Seattle. It was that way all across the country—people celebrating democracy and the power they have because of it.

SPILLS, OIL AND CASH

The biggest corporation, like
the humblest private citizen, must be held
to strict compliance with the will of the
people as expressed in the fundamental law.

—Theodore Roosevelt, 1902

An Act of God?

Ironically, without much time to catch my breath, there was a gigantic oil spill from a tanker, the *Exxon Valdez*, in pristine Prince William Sound in Alaska. Prince William Sound was breathtakingly stunning. It was so beautiful that it made me wonder if it's even part of this earth.

When oil drenched the sound's shores, it was an international travesty. It almost didn't matter whose fault it was. More importantly, the devastation would take years—if ever—for Prince William Sound to recover. Television shots of birds and other animals drenched in oil suffocating from within saddened us all.

As soon as the destruction took place, the news came about how something was awry with the tanker that carried the oil. When I came into work, the people answering the phones gave me some exceedingly angry looks. "What?" I asked in puzzlement. We always had gotten along well.

What I found out is that they had been getting inundated with calls. The people were lending their support for an idea announced in a newspaper column that morning. Eric Lacitis, a noted reporter with the *Seattle Times*, wrote a column saying that, "Mike Siegel, the talk host, ought to lead the campaign about the oil spill."

I was still recovering from the pay-raise campaign, but the victory was exhilarating. It took a tremendous amount of work and intensity including a huge outpouring of emotional energy to accomplish what we had. In talk radio, you go with the flow of events. And if it's activist talk radio, it's not enough to complain. You must act to make changes, but it can be exhausting.

Still, there was substantial public pressure to act. Many people in the Pacific Northwest had personally experienced the beauty of Prince William Sound. I took a deep breath and walked into Brian Jennings's office and said, "Brian, are you ready for another one?" He looked up and answered, "I knew you'd do it. There's too much at stake."

The oil spill had spread, and there seemed to be little action being taken to prevent further irreparable harm to the fragile area. A brief investigation into the matter showed that the lack of action was almost purposeful.

Aleyska, the company that did emergency oil-spill cleanup, was owned by the seven major oil companies, including Exxon. These companies, in concert, chose to reduce their costs at Aleyska to save money. They downsized to the point it wasn't effective anymore.

Having discovered this information and in light of published reports that the ship's captain was intoxicated at the time of the accident leading to the spill, I asked listeners to send me a letter telling me what should be done with regard to Exxon.

A second very significant fact was that there was but a single hull on this tanker. That meant that a puncture—any breach of the outside of the tanker—would send potentially millions of gallons of oil flowing into the sea. If this had been a double-hull tanker, there would have been the ability to, in effect, continue with the ship into shore if the outer skin broke. The inner skin would still be intact, and everything would be okay. This was not the case with the *Exxon Valdez*, unfortunately.

The action the people wanted related to a private entity. No member of Congress was willing to take on Exxon. That left it up to environmental groups and talk radio.

More and more evidence of the devastation of Prince William Sound came pouring in. With every passing day, I got more letters at the station. Letter after letter addressed to "Lawrence Rawl, Chairman of Exxon, c/o Mike Siegel at KING radio" made a mountain on my desk.

It became clear that these letters needed to get to the prime offender. I promised the listeners I would personally deliver their letters and their message to Exxon on May 1.

Just like the congressional pay-raise campaign, I went on shows all over the country. Many people had seen the pictures in newspapers or magazines, and some had even seen TV reports of the animals dying, covered in oil. Once again, I asked the nation to send letters to me addressed to the Exxon chairman.

At the time, I really didn't think the response would be so great. I was wrong. Before long I had received over seventy-five thousand letters from people demanding that Exxon be held responsible for the horror that was inflicted upon the environment in Alaska.

The public interest grew. I appeared on Phil Donahue's and Geraldo Rivera's shows discussing the campaign against Exxon and what could be done to prevent any similar tragedy from happening in the future.

There was too much mail to handle by myself or the staff at KING radio. Volunteers from the listeners offered to help. They helped organize efforts across the country and took care of all the arrangements to make sure every letter got delivered.

Exxon was headquartered in New York at the time. A business owner friend of mine in Brooklyn had an employee drive me around for the day. This was a good thing because the bags of letters filled the trunk and the backseat of the car. We probably should have rented a truck just for the letters.

It turned out that my friend knew the principal at a nearby public school that had a special feeling about the oil spill in Prince William Sound. He said the kids wanted to see me before I went to Exxon. It had been years since I was in a classroom. I was happy to go.

We arrived at an inner-city school in Brooklyn where the kids wanted to meet me because they wanted to express their frustration at what had happened. They had brought pictures of baby seals and birds drowning in the oil. They had written their own letters or their own messages on some of the pictures. None of these children had ever seen Prince William Sound in person. I doubted that any of them had ever been outside the city. But they knew what had been done was wrong, and they wanted to be a part of fixing it.

We drove into Brooklyn. I could say that I spoke to the children at the school, but it was I who did the listening. It was an incredibly overwhelming experience. Here were kids who had lived their entire lives on concrete and asphalt, and they understood the problem with Exxon and the industry as well as any adult. The impact from Exxon's mistakes on Prince William Sound was astounding. These Brooklyn kids, thousands of miles away from the destruction, wanted to help.

That meeting with the school children gave me the emotional nourishment I needed to confront one of the most powerful corporations in the world. We got the bags of mail out; CBS, CNN, and others were there to cover it. The driver loaded the mailbags onto a caravan of carts and wheeled them into the Exxon building in Midtown Manhattan. Lawrence Rawl wasn't available, but he got his second in command, company president Lee Raymond, to meet with me. The meeting was scheduled for twenty minutes.

It turned out that I spent an hour with Raymond. Most of the time he was trying to convince me that Exxon had committed no wrong. I pointed out the anger of the people about this, how there should have been better precautions.

I peppered him with questions:

"Why wasn't there a double hull?"

"How could a captain be intoxicated at the wheel with nobody backing him up?"

"Why were the funds to the emergency cleanup company cut so drastically as to render that effort impotent?"

"What was Exxon going to do to repair a lifetime of damage to the environment of Prince William Sound?"

Raymond never answered the questions. He only tried to deflect them.

When we started that campaign, I was concerned that we might not accomplish anything. It's one thing to affect Congress. They're elected officials, and substantial and organized public pressure threatens their positions. Exxon, however, was a massive corporation, one of the largest operations in the world. They could weather most storms.

At 5:00 p.m. every day, I asked people to turn on their headlights for ten seconds to commemorate the loss of the environmental quality and animal life in Prince William Sound. The people wanted Exxon held accountable. But I cautioned the listeners on the air and said, "Look, I don't know what we're going to accomplish here. I've dealt with civic and political campaigns with public agencies and entities at the state and federal levels, but I don't know what we can do about a publicly traded company that is as powerful as Exxon."

I hadn't realized the level of anger against Exxon. Not only did the people make phone calls, write letters, and turn on their headlights in a public demonstration of protest, they used the greatest power a consumer has. They refused to buy Exxon products.

Exxon was concerned and sent a vice president to Seattle on a public-relations tour. He agreed to debate the issue of the spill, Exxon's culpability, and future spill prevention at the City Club. This club was made up primarily of established downtown business people, and they weren't normally as activist as most of my listeners.

It didn't go well for the Exxon VP. He wasn't combative, but he wasn't apologetic either. I couldn't believe his claim that the damage at the sound was an act of God. They were a company who carried the oil, and it was the company's people who caused the destruction. I took my Exxon credit card out of my wallet, grabbed a pair of scissors, and cut up my card in front of the Exxon VP. Handing it to him, I said, "Sir, I can no longer in good conscience spend any money with Exxon."

As a result of all this public pressure, the people had hurt Exxon's bottom line. Exxon was forced to sell all fifty-seven of its stations in the Seattle area because they weren't doing any business. Another direct result of this campaign was the changing of the law. Then president George Bush, from an oil-producing family himself, signed a bill requiring double-hull tankers in United States waters by the year 2010. So either the present ones have to be retrofitted or new ones built. An outer skin break won't cause a problem anymore due to the protection by the inner skin.

It was clear to me that the people had gained a great deal of power. You just don't gain a private meeting with the president of Exxon unless there is a perception you have a strong position. The people had been successful again, and it was partly because talk radio gave them a voice.

The Bucket Brigade

I needed a break! The Northwest is so beautiful that I wanted to see more of it. During the summer of 1990, after the two exhaustive campaigns, I took off for several weeks to Canada. The sights of western Canada—Jasper, Edmonton, Calgary, and Lake Louise—have a special quality. These are sights to truly behold, not to merely describe.

Every few days I would call my program producer, Cremiere Jackson, just to check messages. On my third call, Cremiere said, "Mike, round 3 time."

"What are you talking about, C?" I replied.

Cremiere explained that the S&L bailout had gained much exposure. My fellow KING talk-radio host, John Hinterberger, had written a column in the newspaper about how ridiculous it was for Congress to bail out huge financial institutions just because they made bad loan after bad loan. Moreover, most loans were uninsured, which meant that there was a lesser institutional examination standard. So the opportunity for financial fraud was far greater than in the more heavily regulated banks.

"So what do you mean by round 3?" I asked.

The producer went on to say that John had wanted to start the Bucket Brigade, standing for, "Not with my bucket do you bail out the savings and loans."

When I got back home, I talked with Hinterberger and agreed to get involved. He was a person of strong personal character and deep philosophical convictions. It wasn't normal for him though to get involved as an activist. He asked for my support, and I was honored to work with him.

The issue was that Congress had committed taxpayer money to literally give away to savings and loan institutions that had lost funds as a result of bad loans. Many of these loans were for third-world investments that could not have been insured with federal funds. The entire bailout seemed like the most extreme corporate welfare any of us had ever seen.

I questioned the public's willingness to take on such a complicated political scheme. That didn't mean we wouldn't try.

So we set up three meetings on the bailout in the community and used our shows to discuss the issue. The first meeting was at the Scottish Rite Hall on Capitol Hill in Seattle. We didn't know what was going to happen. All John and I knew was that we were just trying to halt the savings and loan bailout.

Needless to say, we were delighted when we found a packed hall—nearly one thousand people attended that first meeting. The citizens who helped organize the event did a great job. After we all presented our views on the bailout, the Bucket Brigade was born.

And it was a group that worked well as a team.

The second meeting would be the test. Could we hold the interest? Or was this a one-hit wonder?

That second meeting was at a junior high school in Seattle. The results were the same: an overwhelming turnout. Interestingly, we invited the Congressional delegation from Washington State—most of them representing the Seattle area. Only one person showed up—Jim McDermott, from my district in Seattle. He showed up primarily because he hadn't been in Congress when all of this came down and was innocent of any participation in the bailout. He took a lot of heat, people were very angry, and I tried to make the point as moderator that McDermott wasn't in congress at the time. But he took it all anyway. At the end most of the audience thanked him for showing up and remembered the members of Congress who didn't.

The *New York Times* was at the second meeting and made the point that only one (newly elected) member of Congress even bothered to hear the public's views.

Then we held a third meeting at the same school, again inviting the Members of Congress. John and I put a lot of pressure on the members during our shows to get them to show up. This time, Senators Gorton and Adams appeared, as did four or five of the members of the house. I guessed that the embarrassment of the publicity and fear of ballot-booth reprisals encouraged the attendance.

Again, the hall was overflowing with irate citizens. They kept asking, "Why should the public pay for the corruption or negligence in the savings industry and their friends in Congress?" Since the previous meeting, the citizen group in charge of the Bucket Brigade had uncovered the fact that there were members of Congress who appeared to have personal interests in some of the financial institutions being bailed out. Now the issue was really hitting home. With members of Congress protecting their own interests against that of millions of people, it would seem that the public outrage was completely justified.

As a result of those meetings, the Bucket Brigade, led by Seattle small business persons and the general citizenry, thrived. John and I believed this was a citizen-driven organization rather than one driven by talk radio. We (John and I) provided some initial energy, and then citizen involvement at the grassroots level took over from there. Leaders of the Bucket Brigade later became affiliated with a group in Washington, DC, coordinated by Ralph Nader to force Congress to reconsider the bailout. Some even testified before Congress.

The result was unclear. It's not correct to say the Bucket Brigade was a failure. Though the bailout happened, I think it's fair to say that the amount of support Congress gave to the savings and loan institutions and the Resolution Trust Corporation was greatly diminished as result of the efforts of the citizens. This reduction in support saved the taxpayers millions, and once again, the effort spread nationwide.

The overriding lesson was that Congress had tried to hide the inner workings of government—the bailout of friends—from the people. When a grassroots campaign gets wind under its sails though, it's very hard for even government to ignore.

FROM THE FRYING PAN INTO HOT TALK

Publicity is one of the purifying
elements of politics. Nothing checks all the bad
practices of politics as public exposure.

—Woodrow Wilson, 1913

Taking Clear Positions

Desert Storm was brewing, and I had very definite feelings that the US position in the Middle East was in peril.

I have many friends in Israel, and it was extremely clear that Israel is America's strongest ally. My job as a talk-radio host included taking clear positions where I felt strongly myself. Then the public would have its say. Regardless of agreement, as a provocateur of thought, I couldn't be weak in stating my beliefs.

I later found out that during Desert Storm, Steve Clifford, CEO of KING ownership, went to Program Director Brian Jennings and said, "Brian, Siegel's taking his pro-Zionist position. What are we going to do about this?"

Brian said, "Nothing. He's doing his job. I'm not going to dictate his content."

Clifford was troubled, and went to Bob Golucci, general manager. Golucci echoed what Jennings had said. It is important that talk hosts have the ability to discuss issues even if ownership or management disagrees with the position of the host. Otherwise, how could a host maintain any type of credibility with the listeners?

I continued to do my job at KING. Ratings for KING in my time slot tripled in a little over two years after I went on the air. I was even paid extra to extend the program by an hour to make sure an entire block of time (3:00 p.m. to 7:00 p.m.) of the Arbitron ratings was covered, and showed well for the station.

Then one day Golucci called me into his office and said I could no longer talk about Fitzsimons if I wanted to keep my job. He was the police chief I discussed in a previous chapter. In fact, I was going to have to sign a statement that I wouldn't talk about the chief. I was aghast at what I was being told.

This was difficult for me. I had moved all the way across country to take the job. The show was going great. Ratings, as I said, had tripled. My dilemma was either to maintain my professional integrity and refuse to have my content controlled or stay for the money.

I told KING I would continue to do my program as I had been doing.

Not long thereafter, Jack Swanson became general manager of KING. He called me into his office to tell me that I was being let go. Swanson told me when you have ownership in same city as station, you run into problems.

"The owners deal with the kind of people you challenge. They go to cocktail parties with them. They are social friends. They may even have common business interests," he added.

The official reason given by KING at the time was that I was fired because of a drop in the ratings. That was completely ridiculous, and two months later, KVI called. KING lasted only a few years longer. It's too bad because a multitude of voices is better for a community than a very few opportunities for expression. KING's demise meant a constituency of listeners had to find other stations or simply not participate.

Very Hot

I started at KVI in November 1991 and immediately became entrenched in a matter which had been simmering in the community for some time. It surrounded a person named John Babcock, who was reported to be a pedophile.

Frank LaChance, who headed Neighbors Against Drugs, knew some parents in a neighborhood who had told him that Babcock had been molesting children in the area. This was a low-income area and didn't have much political power. The families asked Frank to intercede on their behalf.

The circumstance that seemed mildly interesting at first soon became a ticking time bomb. LaChance showed that there was a pattern of activity over a period of four years that Babcock was always in the area when and where child molestations occurred. These incidents were enumerated to the police on numerous occasions, but nothing seemed to result from these reports.

A Seattle police officer named Lee Gayles was investigating the Babcock case and believed he was getting close to an arrest when all of a sudden he was pulled off the case by Chief Fitzsimons. Gayles said he didn't know why he was taken off, but there were many accusations flying in every direction.

None of the accusations bode well for the police department, and none of the police department's actions were leading to an arrest of an alleged serial child molester.

Eventually, a detective named Mike Chamness was assigned to the case. Nothing happened. No arrest. No information. No apparent investigation.

In the meantime the topic received nearly daily attention on the show. Then one day, Chamness called a program hosted by Chris Bretcher at KING radio and said the entire Babcock case was being blown out of proportion. The discussion led to the accusation by

Chamness that Detective Gayles had been on some type of glory hunt looking for a high-profile arrest.

Gayles heard about the discussion on KING, and a war of words on radio broke out. While it was great for talk radio, it wasn't good for the circumstance. Gayles indicated that Chamness was protecting Babcock and that "there is something more going on." I didn't know what that meant, but the inferences were pointed at Seattle's elected leadership.

One meeting we verified was with Gayles, LaChance, Chuck Pillon, and city council members Norm Rice and Dolores Sibonga discussing what to do with the Babcock situation. Sibonga wanted the investigation to be expanded, but Rice, who was chair of City Council's Public Safety Committee, was opposed. Gayles provided a picture of Babcock in a negligee retrieved from the Babcock home. It had been on a wall where children were. Rice then immediately exited the meeting. Regardless, there appeared to be little information coming from the police department to the community about the progress of catching the child molester(s) in this low-income neighborhood.

While the verbal battles continued, the fear by the parents in the neighborhood magnified. The risk to children was still there. And no party was being held responsible.

Then something very controversial took place. Detective Chamness sought an order or protection against Gayles. Chamness accused Gayles of harassing him and cited Gayles's statements on my show as examples. As Gayles's hearing was approaching, charges and countercharges were flying. On the day of the hearing, outside the courtroom, just before testimony was to begin, witnesses reported Chamness and Babcock in a close conversation looking like they were old friends. The callers to the show later questioned how an investigating detective could be so chummy with the very person he was supposedly investigating for such horrific offenses against children! The entire Gayles-Chamness episode was strange indeed.

The court upheld the order against Gayles but cautioned the police department to concentrate on investigating crime. Gayles was ultimately fired from the Seattle Police Department.

On January 6, 7, and 8, 1992, my shows were completely dedicated to the child-molestation issues in Seattle. We focused on the Babcock case, and this brought more people to the forefront.

By the summer of 1992, parents in the neighborhood who claimed to be eyewitnesses to Babcock's criminal activity came forth. Yet Chamness was trying to talk them out of prosecuting Babcock, they said. These same parents and our inside sources told us that Chamness had omitted damaging background investigation information uncovered by Gayles. Jeff Baird, a King County deputy prosecutor, said that the police report had clearly excluded matters, and the evidence presented couldn't support a prosecution.

In other words, the report was sanitized.

Public pressure mounted. At every council meeting the parents were playing the tapes of the radio programs devoted to the Babcock case. These same tapes were played over and over again on local news reports and at public forums.

Finally, Prosecutor Rebecca Roe was named to investigate the case. John Babcock was indicted and found guilty of twenty counts of sexual abuse of children. He was sentenced to twenty-eight years in prison. An appeals court reduced the convictions to sixteen counts.

John Henry Browne, a prominent criminal defense attorney in the Pacific Northwest, said that Rebecca Roe told him, "Mike Siegel forced me to prosecute this case."

Bill O'Reilly, then the host of *Inside Edition*, came to Seattle to promote the show. He asked me to appear, and at that time I talked with him about the odd investigation. After our conversation, he publicized the matter, making it a national scandal.

Over the next several months, we supplied O'Reilly all the information we had. This very delicate matter was taken to his network's attorneys to make sure they weren't defaming anyone. The reason was that their own investigation found that Seattle mayor, the former city councilman, Norman B. Rice did nothing about the Babcock case even though he knew about it. Police Chief Fitzsimons did nothing about it even though he also knew about it. Essentially, it was inexplicable that Babcock, the pedophile, was protected from prosecution for so long.

Our own investigation had found that on March 9, 1990, Council Member Sibonga sent Mayor Rice a memo asking about the status of the John Babcock case. She was concerned that Lee Gayles, an African-American police officer, had been mistreated by the department due to his pursuit of the Babcock case.

Sibonga told me two years later that Rice never responded to her memo, never protected Gayles, and never tried to stop Babcock from permanently scarring the lives of children. Only the radio program and the voices of the people had forced the prosecution.

Meanwhile, even after Babcock was tried and convicted, the mayor still wouldn't discuss why it took the people to force action on the case. Inside Edition staked out the mayor's house to get some type of response, but the mayor refused to come to the door. The crew said that Rice hid from them every place they looked. They even got a video shot of Deputy Police Chief Joiner turning his back to the camera and shouting over his shoulder that Police Chief Fitzsimons wasn't available for comment. It seemed that the conspiracy of silence continued even after the conviction.

Interestingly, Inside Edition called the Seattle Times for a photo of Chief Fitzsimons, a public official. The Times refused. O'Reilly said later on our program that he never saw a more provincial and protective media of its public officials than in Seattle. The Seattle print media was the least independent he had seen in terms of their relationships with public officials.

After *Inside Edition* ran its piece, eight minutes of a thirty-minute show, the mayor's press secretary delivered the mayor's official response, saying that the entire Babcock matter was overblown. Local *Seattle Post-Intelligencer* columnist Susan Paynter echoed those sentiments in a column the next day. Paynter claimed it was an old story. My immediate question was, How can sexual abuse not properly investigated and prosecuted be an old story? What if it were her child?

The biggest outrage of all was that children were being sexually molested, violated, harmed for life, and the mayor, the police chief, and some of the local media said the matter was overblown.

This was indicative of the endemic conflict I had encountered for years in Seattle with the lack of an independent media. Whether it's Seattle's elected officials or its sports heroes, the Seattle print media at the time seemed protective of its friends without regard to the harm inflicted upon others. The role of the media is to ask questions, to help the public hold the agencies and officials accountable, and act as a spokesperson for people who don't have the ability themselves to question the actions of government, corporations, and others affecting the public interest.

UGLY SECRETS

The State is a collection of officials,
different for different purposes, drawing
comfortable incomes, so long as the status quo
is preserved. The only alteration they are likely
to desire in the status quo is an increase of
bureaucracy and of the power of the bureaucrats.

—Bertrand Russell, 1922

Providing Catharsis

With the Babcock case behind us, I kept getting more calls concerning child molestation. Some callers went so far as to say there was abject tolerance of pedophilia in the area. I had first heard about an organization called NAMBLA (North American Man-Boy Love Association) years before in Florida at WNWS in 1981. I couldn't believe that NAMBLA even existed. A representative from the group came on the show at KVI and defended sexual relations between adult men and underage boys.

The audience was aghast, as was I. As soon as that show was aired, there seemed to be a floodgate of disclosures about activities that I found incredibly abusive. Here are two of the incidents. We received a settlement agreement and copies of cancelled checks paid to an alleged victim in order to keep the victim quiet about pedophile allegations. The perpetrator was Jeff Smith, the Frugal Gourmet. He was a well-known television chef and author.

The victim was now a young adult who had lived with his secret for years. Irrespective of the money paid to him, he felt he needed to talk in public about what happened. Not only was it cathartic for him, but also he believed that there were others like him who had fallen victim to the same predator.

The victim indicated he had taken the story to the local newspapers, but there was no interest.

During the program, another individual called who had been victimized by Smith. Another civil court action ensued, and I understand the cases have been resolved with payments from Jeff Smith.

In the meantime, Smith's program was cancelled as a result of public pressure. The local PBS affiliate called me asking for advance warning on when we were going to "take on" somebody related to their programming because their phone lines were jammed with irate callers.

The point of even airing this material is that there was, yet again, an example of provincialism—of protecting local celebrities—by Seattle's two daily newspapers. After the program was first aired, I did get a call from both papers. They asked for copies of the backup documentation, which I offered to provide.

The story ran in the papers two years later, long after other victims had come forward. The opportunity for the local print media to be of service to victims had long since passed.

Some may say that it's a difficult task to publicize something about a celebrity. In this instance, the identity of the offender was irrelevant. There were victims out there—innocent victims who as children have had their lives forever scarred. Hiding the truth certainly didn't help those victims. Fortunately, talk radio was in a position to help give some relief to those who could find assistance nowhere else.

OK Boys Ranch

The OK Boys Ranch was a home for at-risk youth. It was licensed by the state Department of Social and Health Services (DSHS) and located near the state capital at Olympia, Washington.

A local civic club, which operated the ranch, gave a genuine good-faith effort to try to have a place for kids to go who didn't have a home and who were subject to the difficulties of life in the street.

We received information of reports to the DSHS of incidents of sexual abuse of boys at the OK Boys Ranch. In fact, we found out later that it had been going on since the 1970s. An attorney for one of the boys found evidence of abuse had been presented to DSHS for years. But the state agency in charge of the protection of children failed to act.

The information about abuse kept coming to us, and we went into the stories on the air in some detail. DSHS had a subagency called the Office of Special Investigations (OSI). It was supposed to review matters relative to DSHS activities. Bowing to public pressure, the DSHS asked OSI to review the OK Boys Ranch.

We were fortunate to have a source close to DSHS, who kept us apprised of the ongoing investigation. We discovered that two of the OSI's people who were looking into the allegations at the ranch were fired on the same day. A person losing a job is an everyday occurrence, but these two investigators believed they were fired because they were getting too close to the truth.

They reported that there was irrefutable evidence that counselors and older youths were regularly abusing young children at the ranch. In a bizarre twist, one man donated land to the ranch.

Then he showed up spending weekends with some of the children.

The frustrating part is that nothing was being done about DSHS and its involvement at the OK Boys Ranch. DSHS's own investigative arm documented that past abusive activities had taken place at the ranch, but DSHS refused to act. The state license of the ranch to operate a boys' home never seemed in peril.

Legislators and my staff contacted the attorney general, who said that nobody at DSHS could be prosecuted because the statute of limitations had expired. Had the DSHS looked into the events when they first happened, perhaps something could have been done.

Then we found that the DSHS supervisor over the OK Boys Ranch knew what had been happening and indicated the ranch was going to cause serious problems for the agency. The DSHS supervisor chronicled his knowledge in a memo sent to Jean Soliz, the secretary of DSHS, only a short time before. But Sid Sidarowicz, the secretary's second in command, never turned that letter over to Soliz. Instead he chose to bury information.

Sidarowicz's answer to criticism was that he didn't think it was "that important." He added that he had been at DSHS for twenty-five years and had seen many letters.

Callers to the show were incredulous. "How could anyone see that kind of letter from an employee exposing dramatic problems and not have acted?" was the overwhelming sentiment.

As the public pressure mounted, the investigation into not only the OK Boys Ranch but DSHS's activities exploded. All along, we kept reporting about these matters, and nothing would ever seem to get done about it. We kept getting calls from employees who asked not to identify themselves saying, "Thank you for doing what you're doing. If you hadn't kept hounding, none of this would have ever come up."

I became highly critical of Soliz. She seemed to be the epitome of an insider whose job came from patronage. The more we looked into DSHS, the more it seemed that the agency was the dumping ground for patronage jobs.

The attorney general was brought in to handle possible prosecutions for either criminal or civil sanctions. Multiple civil lawsuits were brought against the ranch for abuse of children and the state for failing to act in the face of evidence of the abuse. During the litigation, it was found that a DSHS employee had actually sanitized computer files to divert the investigators of OSI. When this extermination of computer files was discovered, it was just the tip of the iceberg at the agency.

The ranch did lose its license and closed. Jean Soliz resigned as director of DSHS, acknowledging that she handled the job ineffectively.

A state court in Washington levied a fine of over $400,000 against the DSHS for its actions and inactions relating to the OK Boys Ranch. And state taxpayers were ordered to pay over $35 million to victims of the abuse.

The OK Boys Ranch was having serious sexual-abuse problems, and people in authority were looking the other way. Because of the complete and systemic incompetence of DSHS management, there were many calls to break up DSHS. Politicians protected this palace of patronage for a while, but the pressure continues to this day to assure that abuse of children is never overlooked again.

The OK Boys Ranch story showed the extent to which entrenched people in government will go to protect its agencies even at the expense of young people. None could seriously argue that any individual at DSHS wanted to harm children. But this agency went to the extreme of looking the other way. The only ones protected were the jobs of those who never prevented the damage from happening in the first place.

TAKING THE INITIATIVE

> We will have to repent in this
> generation not merely for the vitriolic words
> and actions of the bad people, but for the
> appalling silence of the good people.
>
> —Martin Luther King, 1963

Direct Engagement

A big part of my show at KVI from 1991 to 1996 was geared to exposing wasteful government expenditures. I had found and have described in earlier chapters efforts by some legislators and other members of government to sneak through legislation outside the scope of public oversight. I believed that my program acted as a springboard for citizen knowledge and input.

Just before I went on the air at noon one day, I learned from Bob Williams, president of the Evergreen Freedom Foundation, about a hurriedly prepared proposal to build a day care center for employees of the Washington State Department of Labor and Industries. The center was going to cost the taxpayers $1 million to build and then would be free for those state employees using it. And the proposal was going to be considered by the legislative committee that afternoon.

I couldn't believe the audacity of legislators who were willing to spend taxpayers' money in such a cavalier fashion. Working people have to pay for their own day care, and now they were going to have to pay to build a day care center for state workers. In addition, the taxpayers were going to have to pay for the state employees' children to attend. It was outrageous!

The absurdity to me wasn't the proposal itself. While I did feel that employee-sponsored day care may be a good program, such an expenditure should have been under collective bargaining or after careful evaluation by all involved. Here, there was every indication that the state legislature was going to approve this funding without any concern for the people who were paying the bills. So it wasn't the proposal itself. It was the process of excluding the people from the discussion.

I opened the show with the story and gave out phone numbers for committee members. The phone lines to the legislative plaza were soon flooded. The committee hearing scheduled for that same night was cancelled. A few days later, the head of the Department of Labor and Industries sent me a copy of a letter he had sent to the legislative committee chair. He asked that the proposal be withdrawn.

This was major success for the people. It wasn't about the million dollars. Even at that time, $1 million was a mere pittance to state government. The people's victory was to let the legislature know that at every step of the way, the citizens were paying attention. Inappropriate and wasteful government spending was now under the watchful eye of the public.

Initiatives 593, 601, 602

The state of Washington is different from many other states in that the citizens are permitted to write legislation through an affirmative popular vote via an initiative. A certain number of signatures of reg-istered voters is required for the initiative to get on the ballot. The process was intended to give the public a voice when the legislature is deemed to not being responsive.

Crime and government waste were big issues in Washington State in the early 1990s, and we covered both topics extensively on my show.

A bill had been written that would have denied parole rights to offenders with three convictions of certain heinous crimes. The intent was to make it known that repeat offenders were not going to be allowed to stay on the streets of the state subjecting everyone else to the criminal's life of crime. At the very least, criminals who could not keep from committing the worst of crimes against people were going to spend their lives in prison.

For some reason the bill was moving at a snail's pace through the legislature. We talked about it repeatedly on the show. The listeners seemed to be nearly unanimous in their support for the bill, but State Senator Nita Rinehart, who chaired the State Senate Judiciary Committee, kept stonewalling. Instead, she came up with her own watered-down proposal and presented it to her cronies.

Then State Representative Les Thomas called me on the air one day and said he had just attended a meeting of legislators near the airport to discuss several pending bills. Of the dozen members there, he was the only Republican. The considerations among the legislators concerned passage of the bills and how that could be done. Thomas said on the air on my program that Senator Rinehart told the group about a particular bill: "We can get the bill past the public, but how do we get it past Siegel?"

I don't know if this related to the weak bill she proposed in response to "three strikes," but the listeners were outraged that a public official exhibited such utter disregard for the people.

When we looked into the almost spineless Rinehart bill, the people came unglued. Ultimately, the "three strikes and you're out" bill died because the committee chair wouldn't permit a vote. The legislative session ended without action.

Needless to say, the people were angry. They were angry about crime. They were angry that their needs were being avoided through manipulation of the legislative process. They were angry enough to act.

John Carlson, then of the Washington Institute for Policy Studies, and State Representative Ida Ballisiotes, whose daughter had been murdered in Seattle, drafted an initiative: I-593. They hoped this would be the nation's first "three strikes and you're out" law.

John called me and asked for help. He said, "Mike, you can help people pass this law where the legislature refused. Will you get involved?"

I eagerly agreed and led the media effort regarding the initiative. John championed the cause around the state, doing a wonderful job. He has since become a talk-show host on KVI himself and a national leader on the "three strikes and you're out" issue and in passing initiatives.

The initiative garnered substantially more than enough signatures to put it to the ballot. On election day, the "three strikes and you're out" initiative received 75 percent of the vote. This passage was by one of the highest percentages of any election in quite some time.

The concept of "three strikes and you're out" was neither a conservative nor liberal cause. In his next State of the Union address, President Clinton made his own similar proposal, and the state of California went on to pass a similar version.

What the state legislature had arrogantly refused to do, the people of Washington readily passed. In fact, Washington was the first state to pass such a law.

At about the same time, the people were extremely tired of the state government spending hard-earned tax money without accountability.

For example, Washington State's efficiency in education spending was atrocious. The American Legislative Exchange Council, a nonpartisan group, found that Washington State ranked forty-ninth of fifty in percentage of money spent on public education that actually got to the classroom. At the same time, local schools around the state increased their efforts to pass more school bonds, thereby increasing spending without accountability. As a former public school teacher myself, I was appalled.

In the previous year, the highest tax increase in state history had been passed. The citizens were more than angry. They were ready to take government into their own hands.

Two spending limitation initiatives were proposed. One was I-601, a truly grassroots proposal intended to limit government spending in the future on the basis of inflation and population growth. It had been proposed by a state representative, Linda Smith. The campaign was headed by a farmer, Judy Nix.

The other spending limitation initiative was I-602, which was conceived and funded by big corporate landowners and industries that were hurt by the tax increases. They were going to roll back the increases.

I-601 was by far the preferable initiative because it was a true people's campaign. Small businesses were involved like never before.

Judy Nix would come on my show every day to give a five-minute 601 progress report. She would give out addresses of businesses that had the petitions ready for signatures. We simulcast across the state on several occasions. So not only was it a people's campaign, but I-601 also became something important for local radio stations. Most small-town stations were small businesses themselves. They wanted the state to live under constraints just like they had to do. The taxpayers were not a bottomless pit of cash for state government to spend.

I was asked by the leaders of I-602 to meet in Seattle to consider becoming the spokesperson for the initiative. They proposed to send me to meetings, forums, and conferences throughout the state to discuss the I-602. I agreed on the condition that I could speak about I-601 as well, but they weren't keen on that idea. They wanted me to ignore I-601. I even got the impression they were seeking to undermine I-601 because they thought it would give people an either-or choice.

I stood fast that I would only speak for I-602 if I could speak for I-601 as well. They reluctantly said okay, and the campaign got into full swing.

It turned out that I was better for I-601 on radio, letting Judy Nix and others speak about this initiative. As I said before, this was truly a grassroots campaign, and for me to get too involved in the field could detract from the real grassroots nature of the initiative. I continued to talk about it, but I let others be the official spokespersons.

Pat Robertson's Christian Broadcasting Network came to Seattle to film the story about I-601 and the Washington State citizens' initiative process in general. I was asked to be a guest on the show to discuss the public's involvement. The exposure of the government accountability aspect of I-601 on a national network made it an easy decision. I was definitely willing to appear on the show to talk about how the people of Washington State were changing government through initiatives and activism.

The campaigns soon dove into the morass of partisan politics. The Washington Education Association, an NEA affiliated union, poured thousands of dollars and man-hours against the initiatives. WEA leaders wanted to make sure there were no limits on spending or on the amount of money that could be extracted from the people. The WEA even used school property in the campaign, a clear violation of law. This fact was pointed out on numerous occasions to Attorney General Christine Gregoire.

The attorney general sat on her hands and refused to do anything about the violation of law. Eventually, as a result of a private lawsuit, the WEA received the largest fine in state history to that point for campaign law violations. Once again, the people had to take government into their own hands to enforce the law that the attorney general was charged by the State Constitution to enforce.

On election day, the people approved I-601 and denied I-602. A new era in state spending accountability was born. But ever since that day, politicians and special-interest groups with their hands in the taxpayers' pockets have been seeking to find ways around the law. Only through a watchful citizenry can the law be upheld.

VICTIMS OF WENATCHEE

Facts are stubborn things;
and whatever may be our wishes, our
inclinations, or the dictates of our passions, they
cannot alter the state of facts and evidence.

—John Adams, 1770

The Worst Case of Abuse

"If it weren't for Mike Siegel, the families of Wenatchee, Washington, would have never had an opportunity for justice."

This bold statement was made on countless occasions in Washington State and two years later by national media covering one of the worst cases of abuse by any governmental agency in recent history.

From 1994 to 1996, at least sixty men and women were investigated with nearly thirty thousand counts of child sexual abuse. Forty-three adults were arrested, most of them women. A high percentage of the accused was either living in poverty, developmentally disabled, or foreign born and couldn't speak English. Six defendants were convicted at trial, another sixteen pled guilty with Alford pleas, and still another six pled guilty to misdemeanors. (An Alford plea is where the defendant maintains his innocence but admits that he would probably have been found guilty if the case had gone to trial.) The original cases also had four acquittals after trials, and ten cases were dismissed. Ultimately, the eighteen people sent to prison in the cases all have been released. Their convictions were overturned on appeal, or they accepted postconviction agreements to plead guilty to lesser charges during appeal.

Dr. Phillip Esplin, a forensic psychologist and senior research consultant with the National Institute of Health's Child Witness Project, studied the case and said, "Wenatchee may be the worst example ever of mental health services being abused by a state, its social workers and hired therapists, to control and manage children who have been frightened and coerced into falsely accusing their parents and neighbors of the most heinous of crimes."

I have been given a great amount of credit for bringing the awful truths to light about the gruesome treatment that the parents received in Wenatchee. In a way, I am proud to have been able to help bring the truth to light. But the entire Wenatchee sex rings case, as it was initially known, took a heavy toll on all who touched it.

These children will suffer their entire lives as a result of this travesty. But instead of taking credit myself, I tip my hat to the listeners who called upon legislators, government staffers, and media to do something to give back the lives so wrongfully harmed. The listeners may have heard the grim details first on my show, but their actions paved the way for some semblance of justice to later be served.

Throughout this book I have given accounts of how shows that I hosted provided opportunities for the public to impact legislation or policy. The Wenatchee sex rings case was so horrific that it is important for all readers to understand the facts in much the same way the listeners to my show heard the information.

The *Wenatchee World* newspaper stated, "The scope of the Wenatchee wrongful convictions is unprecedented in Washington and perhaps in the country."

That was no overstatement.

Picking out People to Target

The notations below include public facts presented in detailed reports by Kathryn Lyon, Olympia–Washington attorney and author of *The Wenatchee Report*; the American Civil Liberties Union; the Center for Religious Tolerance; WGBH's documentary program for *Frontline*, a PBS production; and my own show. Here is just a glimpse of the shocking story.

Wenatchee is a picturesque community in Central Washington. The drive to Wenatchee from Seattle takes you through two parallel mountains protecting the Columbia River, which sliced through the hillsides centuries before. It is the host of the Apple Blossom Festival in the summer, when the city swells by double. It is the home of large families of migrant agricultural workers, mostly economically disadvantaged Hispanics, and some of the prettiest fruit orchards you would ever see.

But hell came to this friendly small northwestern town in 1994 because of local police and state social service workers.

The parents in the Wenatchee sex rings case were alleged to have committed literally thousands of acts of abuse upon sixty children. A total of seventeen of these children were ripped from their homes and placed for adoption in the hopes of landing with foster families. Contact with the only parents they had ever known was virtually prohibited.

In early 1994, Detective Bob Perez of the Wenatchee Police Department was appointed to investigate crimes against children. This appointment was in spite of the fact that he had a history of petty crimes and domestic strife. In addition, a dismal 1989 police-department evaluation described Perez as having a "pompous, arrogant approach." Further, the police evaluation five years prior said Detective Perez appeared "to pick out people and target them."

At about the time of his assignment as the crimes-against-children investigator, Perez himself became the foster parent of a young girl. Not long thereafter Perez sought out the poor, developmentally disabled, racial and ethnic minorities of Wenatchee and "began aggressively questioning both children and adults."

The interrogations of adults typically were reported to have involved "deprivation of sleep, food, or breaks; repeated leading questions; use of threats and intimidations; use of promises or incentives; profanity; derision and name-calling; officer's unyielding expectation of guilt and refusal to accept contradictory information." Other documented aspects of the interrogations included threatening the parents and other adults with "life imprisonment, ugly death in confinement, and the certainty of never seeing their loved ones again."

Many confessions were ultimately obtained; some of which were written in language "far beyond the mental capacity" of the particular defendant. Almost all of the confessions were recanted after the interrogation sessions had ended. These people were coerced into confessions, were low income, many non-English speaking and did not have adequate legal representation. They became targets of abuse by public officials in Wenatchee.

Nearly simultaneously, Detective Perez was interrogating children as well. The children received, essentially, the "facts as known" by the police. Then, allegedly, the children were threatened "with detention or immediate arrest of their parents if they didn't tell" of the abuse already "known."

Many of the children were eventually transferred out of state or into mental wards. One source wrote, "Children who failed to cooperate or who recanted their statements were isolated from all extended family, schools, churches, friends, and neighborhoods; placed in recovered memory therapy; subjected to courses of powerful psychotropic medication; and placed in mental health facilities where the apparent focus of treatment was extracting information of child abuse."

The case even had economic implications that could have been disastrous for the state of Washington.

The justice committee of San Diego had been organized by people who were concerned about the Wenatchee problem. They called for a national boycott of Washington State's principle product: apples.

The justice committee issued a statement in late 1995:

The purpose of the boycott is to bring to the attention of citizens, civic groups and officials in Wenatchee and state officials in the

State of Washington, the national outrage over the false prosecutions and the civil rights abuses suffered by both children and adults as a result of the child abuse investigations and prosecutions which began last year and continue unabated...Despite a call by Washington Governor Mike Lowry and House Speaker Clyde Ballard for a U.S. Justice Department investigation of the Wenatchee prosecutions, local police and prosecutors have persisted in pressing these outrageous cases.

Throughout this case, I broadcast shows and reports about the events in Wenatchee. State government could have—should have—intervened. The calls for federal intervention from Governor Lowry and Representative Ballard (R-E. Wenatchee) were attempts to divert attention. Instead of seeking federal assistance, I questioned why they, as leaders of the state government, didn't do something themselves! In fact, Ballard refused to hold hearings in Wenatchee, saying that if the people of the area wanted hearings, they could go to Yakima (a city about two hours away).

State Representative Dale Foreman (R-Wenatchee), Statehouse Majority Leader, proved to be of no help. I wondered where he was, why he was absent, and if he would ever show some leadership. He was a well-educated, capable person and lived in the city where the witch hunts were taking place. He simply refused to stop the senseless plunder by the police and social workers, even stating on my show that he couldn't get involved in the cases because he was part of the potential trial jury pool.

With Ballard and Foreman refusing to hold hearings in Wenatchee giving the local people a voice, I asked Pastor Roberson if the local citizens wanted to be heard. He enthusiastically replied yes!

Roberson felt that allowing the people to speak in public would help them deal with the tremendous mental trauma they were undergoing. The purpose of the meeting would be to permit people to have their say about the investigation, child abuse allegations, and others.

I announced on my program that such a meeting was going to be held in Wenatchee. State Senator Pam Roach, who was from an area just outside Seattle, must have heard the show because she called and asked to participate. Finally, someone from state government wants to get involved.

Then I called newly elected Chelan County commissioner Earl Marcellus (from Wenatchee) and Kathryn Lyon, the Olympia attorney, to join the panel listening to the public.

Since I had announced the meeting several days ahead of time that I was going to broadcast the voices of the people direct from Wenatchee, I became very concerned for my own safety. The history of the Wenatchee investigation was that it seemed whoever was critical of the Wenatchee police then became a target. I announced I would be driving over but booked a flight to the small Wenatchee airport. Having already arranged for protection when I arrived, we still took back roads to the meeting hall.

The outpouring of emotion at the hearing is something that will remain with all who attended for the rest of their lives. Friends and family members cried for their children. Many were confused because they didn't understand the language well. They were angry. They were afraid. I'm told the broadcast marked a turning point in the public's resolve to fend for themselves and gave hope that help would be there to get their children back.

Formulating the charges

Very early in the investigation, long before more facts became known, and before any of the Wenatchee sex rings defendants had been charged, an adolescent girl was in detention at the local juvenile hall. She was visited by Detective Perez. After several hours alone with Perez, the girl told Perez that her foster father had been abusing her for years. That same day, Perez arrested the father and charged him with numerous counts of sexual abuse.

The next day, the young girl's juvenile caseworker, Paul Glassen, visited her. "I feel really bad," she told Glassen. "This police officer was, like, trying to set Dad up or something. He made me say a whole bunch of lies."

Glassen was uncertain of what the truth was and submitted a detailed report to his supervisor. The report included the girl's allegations against Perez. Glassen's supervisor gave the report to Perez. The next day, Perez arrested Glassen for "tampering with a witness." Glassen was immediately placed on "administrative leave" and later fired.

One of the main defendants, Reverend Roby Roberson, was the pastor of the East Wenatchee Pentecostal Church of God House of Prayer. This church was the pit of evil to Detective Perez. Many of the targets of the Perez investigation attended Roberson's church.

Roberson believed that improper police investigations involving some people in his congregation were being conducted and that claims of child molestation were unfounded. He began to question the police and social agencies about the investigation. Roberson was particularly outraged when Harold Everett, a church member, was arrested, partially on the basis of Everett's own written statement. Roberson knew that Everett could neither read nor write and complained vehemently to the prosecutor.

Roberson spoke publicly for the first time about his concerns over the child-sex-rings investigations at a community forum on March 23, 1995. By that time, the issue had become so onerous in Wenatchee that the meeting was televised locally.

Shortly after that meeting, Roberson and his wife, Connie, found that they were targets of an investigation themselves. They were arrested fourteen days later and charged with twenty-two counts of raping and molesting children. Their young daughter was taken away too.

Pending trial, the Robersons were sent to the county jail, where they spent 155 days and nights. They were unable to raise the funds necessary to post the $1 million bail.

After a more detailed investigation by Perez, all twenty-two counts were withdrawn but were replaced by a set of new charges involving a completely different child not previously mentioned!

The Robersons fought on. From jail, Robbie Roberson appeared on my show describing the circumstance in Wenatchee. I'm sure his lawyer, Robert Van Siclen, advised against these appearances, but the pastor was adamant about getting the truth out.

On December 11, 1995, the Robersons were acquitted of all fourteen charges of abuse. Reports indicated that some of the jurors were angry at the prosecution for bringing a case to court without any real supporting evidence.

Shortly thereafter, Roberson appeared on my program from his home. Just before the show ended at 6:00 p.m., his wife, Connie, brought their daughter into the house. This was the first time he had been able to see his daughter in all that time. I closed down my microphone and let the show end with Pastor Roberson crying tears of joy.

In the meantime, Glassen, by then a former juvenile caseworker, heard that he had become Perez's latest target. He immediately fled to Canada with his Canadian-born wife and their five-year-old son.

"I knew what they could do to my son," Glassen said. "And I wasn't going to let Perez or anybody else start brainwashing him or God knows what."

Fighting Back

Roberson continued in his appearances on my show. Trials were expensive, and I gave him a forum to raise funds to defend the Wenatchee defendants. But it wasn't going to be enough. In the meantime, the listeners were busy making calls to legislators and media to bring about attention to the cases. CBS, CNN, NBC Dateline, the Wall Street Journal, and the Washington Post all did stories critical of the Wenatchee sex rings cases, but the government did nothing. And the prosecutions continued.

Another of the defendants, Donna Rodriguez, a friend of the Robersons, went on the attack herself. In her case, Detective Perez questioned Donna Rodriguez's then ten-year-old daughter after pulling her out of school. Perez grilled the little girl for four hours and threatened to arrest her mother unless the girl admitted to sex orgies with various adults, including her mother. The child later said she was terrified of Perez and that he was shaking her. She specifically recalled Perez telling her, "You have ten minutes to tell the truth."

Perez then wrote out a two-page statement for the girl to sign and told her she would be able to go home when she signed the statement. The girl signed the paper, and Perez immediately went to arrest and jail Rodriguez. The little girl didn't see her mother again for six months. Rodriguez hired a lawyer, and two days before her trial was to begin, prosecutors dropped all 168 counts against her.

Pastor Roberson continued to expose the acts of the Wenatchee police and social agencies. The cases gained more notoriety, and the University of Washington formed the Innocence Project Northwest. This new organization brought the resources of the prestigious UW law school to Wenatchee. Other public-interest lawyers also started helping the people defend themselves.

Ultimately, the law teams, with mounting public pressure, brought the Wenatchee sex rings investigation to an end and set in motion the means to get all the wrongly accused people out of prison.

The Robersons increased their own attack and filed several civil lawsuits. In one case against the state, the Robersons and two wrongfully charged people received a settlement of $850,000.

The Robersons (and three others) filed a multimillion suit against the city of Wenatchee and several officials for negligent investigation and for violations of federal civil rights (42 USC 1983). This is one of the first suits of its kind where, as a result of a unanimous ruling by the Washington State Supreme Court, the Wenatchee police find themselves unable to use the shield of immunity to prevent consideration of liability.

There was a dismissal and reinstatement and a $700,000 assessment against the city of Wenatchee for failing to comply with pretrial discovery. This may be one of the largest assessments of its kind.

Regardless of the outcome of the Roberson lawsuit, money will not change the horror that has been inflicted upon them and their family. In an editorial dated September 18, 2000, the *Seattle Times* said it well: "These four—and the other victims of this thoroughly discredited investigation and its rogue cop perpetrator—can never be compensated for the emotional and spiritual damage inflicted on them. Those who allowed it to happen can and should compensate them for the financial damage done."

To this day, I cannot understand how then US Attorney General Janet Reno could state in February 1996, "These complaints [of abuse by the police, prosecutors, and social agencies] do not present evidence of prosecutable violations of federal civil rights law."

I cannot understand why the state's leaders failed to exercise the leadership to investigate whether the citizens of the state were being victimized by government action. Once again, state government leaders protected themselves, not the people. Anyone who reads about the events of the Wenatchee sex rings case will be utterly appalled at how people—both adults and children—were treated.

It is an obligation of the media to expose wrongs and the impairment of the human condition. It wasn't risky at all to discuss what was happening in Wenatchee. We didn't need history to prove that. I am still completely dismayed as to why the leading print media is the state, the *Seattle Times* and *Seattle PostIntelligencer*, failed to even cover the events in Wenatchee until nearly two years after the children and adults had been forever harmed. Had those newspapers been responsible and helped expose what was happening in Wenatchee, many people's lives could be better today.

This is a case where the acts of commission and omission by government were so atrocious that innocent lives have forever been ruined. This was a sad, sad occurrence where there were victims—simply only victims.

ON BECOMING A LOCAL

Every now and again take a good look
at something not made with hands—a
mountain, a star, the turn of a stream. There
will come to you wisdom and patience
and solace and, above all, the assurance
that you are not alone in the world.

—Sidney Lovett, ca. 1960

Building a Field

In the summer of 1995, the city was electric. It was because of the Seattle Mariners. Ken Griffey provided the power. Edgar Martinez rained doubles. Randy Johnson struck out, well, everybody, and a young Alex Rodriguez patrolled shortstop. The team was the best in franchise history.

But Mariners management wanted a new stadium. The Kingdome had served the team well, but this was a different era. To have an appropriate place for baseball, there needed to be a state-of-the-art outdoor ballpark.

Mariners's management threatened to either sell the team or take it to another city if a new stadium wasn't built. They wanted taxpayer support. Several state legislators agreed and tried to put together a funding package inside state government. There was too much public opposition though. Instead, the legislature authorized King County, Washington, to submit a construction and funding plan to the voters.

I grew up a Brooklyn Dodger fan. I know what a great baseball park means to a region. I still remember the day I heard that my beloved Dodgers were moving to Los Angeles.

I supported the new stadium wholeheartedly. Many of my listeners and friends disagreed. They called the proposed stadium corporate welfare. I countered with the fact that a thriving baseball team with a good park would bring millions of dollars to the area—and would be worth every taxpayer penny.

To make the point of the impact of a new stadium on a city, I convinced KVI to let me broadcast my show live from the new Coors Field in Denver and Jacobs Field in Cleveland. A plum assignment indeed!

The public vote was barely defeated. The state legislature convened a special session. US senator Slade Gorton (R-WA) helped bring the parties together. In heated debates, the state legislature approved funding for the ballpark that would eventually become Safeco Field.

This wonderful facility, born in controversy, has in only a few short years proved its worth to the community.

Norm in the Temple

I love Seattle for its natural beauty. The views are virtually unsurpassed anywhere else in the world. The waters of the lakes that surround Seattle or the Puget Sound, which extends even farther, provide echoes of sunsets that draw artists to paint masterpieces. The nearby mountains are inviting enough to appear friendly, ominous enough to be respected.

But I do not love Seattle for its local government.

It is not true that I do not like Norm Rice. He's affable and certainly would be an acquaintance with whom to watch a college football game. But Norm Rice sought and received the public trust, first as a council member and then as mayor of Seattle.

The job of media, especially talk radio, is to ask questions and expose wrongs. That requires the challenge of authority. The power elite who control Seattle do not like its minions being confronted. Norm Rice was one of those minions controlled by the powers. Under Norm Rice's tenure as mayor, Seattle became known as the king of corporate welfare, and it is no wonder that Seattle has some of the highest taxes in the nation.

From 1993 to 1996 I received numerous reports of Rice being involved in a shooting altercation. Though the allegations were made in writing, I had never addressed them on the air. Instead, I chose to seek independent verification.

I didn't receive corroborating evidence and basically tried not to think about the allegations. That was difficult though. I was recognizable around the city, and whenever I would go to a restaurant, a movie, or grocery shopping, I would often get stopped and asked about Rice and the shooting. My consistent response was that I had not been able to prove it and am waiting for someone with direct knowledge before I would go on the air.

Many of these people were employees of the city and wanted Rice out of office. But I was more concerned about the use of taxpayer money for private projects and the blatant waste of money inside the administration of Mayor Norman B. Rice.

Rice as mayor led Seattle to being one of the most inefficient cities in the nation. When I moved to the Puget Sound in the late 1980s, the streets were clean, the potholes were filled, and the pride of the citizens was clear. But by 1996, the city had become a haven for homeless people who were allowed to take over parts of downtown. The streets looked cluttered, and longtime resident friends of mine were wondering, "Who loves Seattle anymore?"

The city auditor acknowledged that the city had one of the worst supervisors-to-employee ratios in the country. In some instances, a supervisor would have only one employee to manage while retaining a hefty salary. Under Rice, Seattle became a patronage haven rivaling 1930s Chicago.

I strongly supported Rice's opponent in 1994. Rice won handily. My support through KVI clearly didn't help the opponent. My show was popular in Seattle from the ratings standpoint but didn't influence voters in Seattle enough to help defeat Rice. Outside Seattle was a different story, but people outside Seattle didn't vote for mayor.

In 1996, Rice chose to run for the Democratic nomination for governor. He had a record in office on which to run, and I was going to discuss it on my show. I was known around the state on radio since I had worked on initiative campaigns. My past involvement meant I was a guest often on programs in Eastern Washington and in Vancouver, Washington, as well as in Western Washington, where I lived. That meant I had relationships with stations across the state.

Since this was a statewide campaign, a number of radio stations in Washington state wanted to have simulcasts with my program about political races affecting their audiences. This allowed listeners in both cities to hear the program at the same time and learn about each other's political campaigns. One of the stations was from Spokane, KGA, and its host, Richard Clear.

In April 11, 1996, we held a joint broadcast on KVI and KGA with Richard Clear hosting from Spokane, and I hosted from Seattle. The primary issue of that show was Norm Rice's candidacy for governor. We had callers from both sides of the state, asking questions, making comments, mostly critical. I was certainly critical of Rice's performance as mayor and gave the opinion that he wasn't qualified to be governor.

Then after the three-hour show was well underway, Richard Clear asked about the rumors of the shooting. He was specific as to the allegations of the facts. I responded that the rumors did indeed exist.

Then I made errors in judgment and allowed the rumors to persist on the show. For years I wouldn't permit them to be stated, but then after they became public on the show, I didn't stop them. I knew I was legally correct in the way I handled the matter, but in retrospect, it wasn't the right thing to do to permit the airing of the rumors.

Rice's campaign consultant, Bob Gogerty, was a brilliant Democratic strategist. The Rice campaign was having difficulties raising money, and this incident could have been perceived as a way to draw attention to his candidacy. A few weeks after the KVI-KGA simulcast, Norm Rice called a press conference to denounce the airing of the rumors.

I believe it was great strategy for the Rice campaign. It provided energy where there hadn't been. I was hurt by one aspect though. The press conference was held at Temple de Hirsch Sinai on May 13, 1996. It was entirely inappropriate for the Rabbi Starr to permit the use of a temple for politics. Even worse was Rabbi James Mirel, who had asked me in the past to speak at the Temple B'nai Torah regarding Judaism's influence on me in social activism, stood at the podium with Rice in a show of pure partisan politics.

What I did in permitting an unsubstantiated rumor to persist on my program was bad judgment. What the rabbi did in bringing politics into the temple, a holy place, was worse.

A firestorm of publicity developed after the press conference. The same print media that wrote scathing attacks of me for allowing the rumors to be discussed on my program then printed more information about the rumors than I had ever heard.

On May 14, 1996, I publicly apologized to Norm Rice and was suspended at KVI shortly thereafter. I received a huge amount of public support, but there was also some applause for the move in the community.

At the end of the month, six weeks after the airing of the program, I was fired by Fisher Broadcasting, the owner of KVI. Within one day, I received four other broadcast job offers and was back on the air within a week.

If I had it to do over again, I would still expose the record of a candidate for public office. But I will never permit an unsubstantiated rumor to be broadcast on my show.

WTO: The Battle in Seattle

After KVI, I worked on a statewide radio network, nationally syndicated shows, and other special broadcasts, which I will address in another chapter. One of my assignments had me covering a large gathering in Seattle now known around the world as the Battle in Seattle. The World Trade Organization had come to town.

The air was filled with tear gas. The streets were manned by armed personnel. It was all to hold the people at bay.

Was this Chicago 1968? Or the Kent State shootings? Could it have been Beirut in the 1970s?

No, it was Seattle—just thirty days from the year 2000.

I took my microphone into a crowd of fifty thousand protesters. The public occupation of the downtown streets went on for hours. As nightfall came, the storm trooper–like police mounted an offensive against the people. The crowd was pushed into the nearby densely populated urban neighborhood of Capitol Hill. People walking their dogs for the evening were treated like looters.

The police plan changed from passive observation to rubber bullets, tear gas, and pushing the people into a nearby residential area. This created total havoc, and I wondered to myself at the time if a trip to the grocery would be a trek into hell. It turned out to be the latter for many local people.

Delegates came from around the world to the Emerald City at the invitation of the city's leaders to celebrate the global economy. In addition to the delegates were people from as far away as New Delhi and as close as down the street, all protesting the oppressive giant monolith of the WTO. The initial police plan was relatively permissive.

The WTO meeting in Seattle was to be the mayor's (Paul Schell) and a Port of Seattle commissioner's (Pat Davis) shining achievement. They were going to show the world our fine city. What a joke! Apparently they completely overlooked violent citizen uprisings surrounding the WTO in Geneva and India. Seattle's Mayor Schell and police chief Norm Stamper (who resigned shortly after WTO) knew that wherever this organization gathers, there was violence. Not only was this information readily available to anyone who could use a computer, but peaceful protest organizers had been warning Mayor Schell for months before the event.

It was fortunate more property wasn't destroyed, more people weren't hurt, and no one was killed.

My purpose was to merely report the reasons for those protesting. Sure, there was an element of gleeful lawlessness among some of the protesters, but I was extremely impressed with many of the young people who knew the implications of WTO proposals so thoroughly.

The interviews from the scene of the WTO riots that day were broadcast on the Talk America Radio Network in national syndication, KTRS in Saint Louis, and World Webcast Network. I was very impressed with the depth of knowledge of some of the protesters. They were articulate, well-informed, and willing to listen to other arguments. This was not what most others in media portrayed.

Trade among nations must take place. As technology helps the world grow smaller, the ability to buy and sell goods across international boundaries is important to the economic health of all cultures. But the WTO didn't seem to be about fairness or protection of the environment or human rights. Instead, the WTO rules were promulgated in secret for the sheer purpose of profit.

Rather than provide reams of information about fair trade, I just want to make the point that well over 90 percent of the people who protested the WTO in Seattle in late 1999 were peaceful activists. The issues they brought forth will not go away with the smoke on the streets. The twenty-first century will see the issues of the environment and human rights at the trade table. If these concerns are not represented at the trade negotiation tables, there will be significantly more violence at future WTOs than there was in Seattle.

ERASING BOUNDARIES

For this generation, ours,
life is nuclear survival, liberty is human rights,
the pursuit of happiness is a planet whose
resources are devoted to the physical
and spiritual nourishment of its inhabitants.

—Jimmy Carter, 1981

Can This Happen Here?

Throughout the years of working with individual stations, I've also hosted at regional stations and on syndicated shows. These are much different than local shows because you cannot allow geographically concentrated issues to dominate a show. That keeps the vast majority of listeners from wanting to participate.

I do have a theory though that local issues in one city are similar to local issues in another area. As a result, if done correctly, local issues can be covered on national shows.

For example, I covered the Wenatchee sex rings case on a nationally syndicated show. Not only were the listeners mortified as to what was happening, they were clearly questioning if this can happen here in their local area.

While we have boundaries that separate our states, counties, and cities, Americans seem to have common experiences, cares, and concerns. As long as I didn't get bogged down in minutia of local nuances, I found that national and other syndicated shows can be done as if right in your own neighborhood.

In 1988, when I was still in New York, I received a call on Thursday afternoon from Rick Sklar at Sun Radio Network in Tampa. He was in a bit of a tight spot because the host, and cofounder of the network, Chuck Harder, had just walked out. Harder and his partner had gotten into a disagreement.

Sklar pleaded with me, "Get on a plane, Mike, now! We need you on the air tomorrow."

I agreed to go. The opportunity was good, and right before I hung up the phone, Rick added, "Oh by the way, Mike, it's a consumer show. Be ready to talk about products and prices."

I hadn't hosted anything like that. But I had almost twenty-four hours to get ready. Instead of going to the airport, I headed to the magazine stand to find the latest materials on the topic. By the time I arrived in Tampa at noon the next day, I was ready. Thank goodness there wasn't a traffic jam from the airport because I went on the air at 3:00 p.m.

When I talked with Rick on the phone, I didn't know how long I was going to stay, but it would be at least a week. For the next week, people from all over the country discussed consumer issues. The show was exhilarating because it wasn't all about government. Instead, it was about everyday matters and how the quality of life could be improved through sharing information.

Some may think that sounds a little bland. In fact, I was very surprised at how defensive people became about their favorite products.

Anyway, the show went very well during that week. Management was extremely happy at the public response. Over that period, Harder and his partner worked out their differences. I returned to New York.

David Rimmer was in charge of programming ABC Radio Network in New York and knew I was a lawyer in addition to being an on-air host. David asked me to host a one-hour legal show called *Legal Lines* on Saturdays. The network had 140 affiliates around the country.

Just about every market has a local legal talk show. Here, the show was national, and since every state has different legal standards, it was very difficult to be specifically responsive. Plus, this was as different show in that it was almost like I was being interviewed by the public. I was the expert. The opportunity for issue engagement just isn't the same as with the talk-show format I preferred.

Interestingly though, in the year I hosted *Legal Lines*, I found that show to be very similar to the week at Sun Radio Network. Legal questions and consumer questions are much the same. It also helped me develop a moniker known to this day as the People's Advocate.

While I've done other syndicated fill-in for Westwood One (Bob Grant Show), for the WOR Radio Network, and for WOR in New York (Joey Reynolds Show), the chance to host my own nationally syndicated show has come my way several times.

I worked for Chancellor Broadcasting company and collaborated with the Business Radio Network. This was a national show that I did while I was with KVI in Seattle. I would do my KVI show in the afternoons and then the national show at night.

My work at Chancellor led me into the Talk America Radio Network, then I headquartered in Boston. My time with Chancellor and Talk America lasted for two and a half years.

The Devil Is in the Details

During the time I hosted the nationally syndicated shows, the bill known as HR 6 was proposed in the US House of Representatives. It was several hundred pages long and was generally thought to be a reauthorization of the previously existing federal education law.

Buried deep within the bill was a single sentence that required all teachers of students below college level to be certified. The uproar over that one sentence was incredible. If passed into law, this bill would have effectively meant any homeschooled student couldn't get a high school diploma. Moreover, the parent of any homeschooled student would have been subject to child neglect and criminal penalties for failing to provide an education for the child.

The bill had bipartisan support, not because of the one sentence, but because it was too thick to read. Similar to the two-thousand-page North American Free Trade Agreement (NAFTA) that was approved by Congress without having been read, the education reauthorization bill was generally considered by house members to require a mere cursory review.

The homeschooling community in the United States was largely based in religious beliefs. Many of these parents believe that the public schools were not providing an appropriate education. So they chose to homeschool, and most homeschooled children received a very high quality academic education.

I neither approve of nor oppose homeschooling. It is a tremendous undertaking by the parents who do it. And not all those who homeschool do so for religious reasons.

In any event, the issue quickly became volatile. Homeschooling parents from around the nation literally jammed the congressional telephone system. The highest number of calls Congress has ever received on an issue was about HR 6, and it was nearly unanimously opposed because of the one lone sentence in the lengthy bill.

My show was by no means the only discussion of this issue. The importance of the HR 6 mobilization was that Americans were empowered, partially through talk radio, to have tremendous impact on legislation. Perhaps it was that the issue directly affected people in their homes in a way that other legislation typically does not, but the people won. The sentence was removed. Homeschooling parents could continue.

I remember getting congratulatory calls for being host of a national show that made a difference. Instead, it was me who should have been congratulating the people. That is a great example of participatory democracy. That is what empowerment specifically is about.

Spanning the State

Andy Skotdal of Everett, Washington, a progressive community about twenty miles north of Seattle, headed KRKO-AM. Andy dreamed of having a statewide network and asked me to be his anchor host.

Andy created the Mike Siegel Network and added twenty-two stations throughout the state of Washington to the network. The network broke new ground in that it limited itself to geographical boundaries of one state.

Like so many states, Washington is made up of a few metropolitan areas and many small towns. A small-town radio station is almost like a member of the family to the local people. These stations were authorized years before by the FCC to provide a vehicle of information to the local people. Often, small-town stations have been owned by the same family for years, and many of them existed in Washington State. But these stations don't have the budgets to compete for national news or to gather regional news. The townspeople do have a strong interest in state issues. That's why so many stations quickly jumped on board with my show, a known quantity in the state.

In many ways, the show educated the two distinct parts of the state about each other. East of the Cascade Mountains is where most of the land of the state is located. The economy is agriculturally based.

West of the Cascades lies the Puget Sound, a heavily urbanized area. People in the two sides of the state often don't agree with each other because they approach issues from entirely different points of reference.

We discussed water problems that Eastern Washington farmers were experiencing. Those farmers wanted concessions that the Western Washington environmentalists believed was damaging. The farmers, who support many workers, countered that they were being economically sabotaged by people who don't understand their daily challenges.

It turns out that there were toxins in fertilizer that was being used on farms in Eastern Washington. The Seattle Times did a lengthy series about this issue. But experts differed on the allegations, and there were claims of mischaracterization. It was found that some of the toxins in the fertilizer were also used in antioxidant vitamins for human consumption. This topic caused Eastern Washington farmers to discuss their use of the fertilizer and ask for advice. You could almost see the farmers shaking their heads and throwing up their hands.

The Washington State Department of Ecology began rationing water to the farmers during a rain shortage in Eastern Washington. Farmers expressed frustration at not being able to get enough water for their crops. They even started a bumper-sticker campaign (on cars, trucks, and tractors) saying No Water, No Food.

I must say that I gained a new respect for farmers and all they go through just to produce food.

The show included a discussion of the impact of the endangered species act, transportation needs, the Hanford Nuclear Power Plant, and many other issues that showed the listeners there were great differences in the needs of the people in the two areas.

I took the program back to Wenatchee and did a recap to see how the people of this lovely small city were recovering. I took the show to different parts of the state to allow the local flavor of each aspect of my beautiful home state to be broadcast throughout.

The many small businesses in the state were particularly interested in a series of programs I did on regulation and taxation. Business owners from around the state called to talk about obscure and bizarre regulations from which they couldn't get relief. We took the matters direct to the legislature through the program right to the state capitol.

From a programming standpoint, the show was a success. The affiliates were extremely happy because they had programming they couldn't otherwise get.

But from the business side, the network struggled. We were challenged by the fact that large advertising buyers are regionally based. This meant that unless the network was expanded outside state borders, regional ad money wasn't available to the network.

That also meant that ad buyers preferred to purchase ads with the local stations for much lower costs. After one-and-a-half years, we suspended operations of the network. Considerations are currently underway to determine how the network can be back on the air. Perhaps, someday, there will be a network covering the entire Pacific Northwest.

QUEST FOR TRUTH

Opinions become dangerous to
a state only when persecution makes it
necessary for the people to communicate
their ideas under the bond of secrecy.

—Charles James Fox, England
House of Commons, 1797

Area 51

It was about ten in the morning, and the phone rang. The voice was that of Kraig Kitchin, president of Premiere Radio Network.

"Mike, you probably don't know this, but for several months we've been auditioning different hosts to take over for Art Bell. You're the best. We want you. We want you, Mike, to take over the third-highest-rated talk-radio show in the nation."

I was stunned speechless—a condition my friends say is an impossibility.

I had guest-hosted Art's show twice preceding this call. At the same time, I'd been doing shows all over the nation—Saint Louis,

Seattle, New York, Boston, Spokane, and a nationally syndicated show. When I had first been called to guest-host for Art Bell, I thought it was just his vacation time. I didn't know I was being auditioned.

Coast-to-Coast (Art Bell's show) was a huge success for Premiere, owned by Clear Channel Communications. Clear Channel is the nation's largest radio broadcasting company, owning nearly 1,200 stations. So the opportunity to host this show was one of those once-in-a-lifetime chances. Art himself was very talented and had worked with the producers, supported by Clear Channel, to build a multi-million audience and successful show. And it was a show with its own distinctive personality plus!

It turned out that Premiere Radio Networks had actually known for about a year that Art Bell wanted to retire. During that yearlong period, Premiere tried about thirty different guest hosts on the program with the goal of finding a new permanent host. I doubt that any of them knew that it was an audition.

I had sent a promotional package to Lowry Mays about a month before related to working with Clear Channel. Being the chairman of the nation's largest radio network, I didn't think he would read it himself, but he did! Rather than contact me directly about opportunities with a Clear Channel affiliate, he sent the material through to Alan Corbeth, senior vice president of Premiere and the only producer *Coast-to-Coast* has ever had.

Alan lives in a small town in Oregon that is also the site of origination of the show. He had heard my work on radio for years, either on national networks, as a guest host, or when he had been in Seattle. He told me later that he was surprised I was asked to guest host *Coast-to-Coast* because my focus had been current events and activism. But after he heard me guest host his show, he said, "I was sold!"

I remember telling Alan jokingly that maybe we could start a citizens' initiative to open the Roswell files.

Kraig said I had two final hurdles to jump: the first was the company president, Randy Michaels, and the second was Art Bell himself. Art and I were old friends. I had tremendous respect for him and his work. I felt like a nervous sprinter ready to get out of the starting block.

I went to Los Angeles that weekend and met with Premiere and Clear Channel representatives for four hours. I passed and a schedule was set for the following Tuesday to go just outside of Area 51—to Art Bell's compound.

We arrived in Las Vegas and then drove to Art's home near Pahrump, Nevada. The road to get there seemed like it was right out of the *X-Files*, and I admit that eeriness added to the nervousness that had been with me since LA.

Because Art values his privacy, I'm not going to go into detail about his home, but I will say that he regards *Coast-to-Coast* like his child. Even though he thought he was ready for retirement, just like a child leaving home for the first time, it would be difficult for Art to hear someone else host *Coast-to-Coast*.

I passed Art's scrutiny and was on my way to being the radio-man for the third-most-listened-to talk-radio show in America.

To those who weren't listeners of *Coast-to-Coast*, the genre of the show was much different than anything I had ever done. The topics of the show included the paranormal, the unusual, and the mysteries of the universe. A show of that type would certainly have interesting guests and even more interesting callers.

The initial transition to hosting *Coast-to-Coast* was difficult because Art Bell and I split the program every week for the next month. Alan and Art wanted there to be a gradual change to the new host. Premiere facilitated the transition very well. This was clearly the most professional broadcast company with which I had ever worked.

In the first few months, there was enormous pressure. The broadcasting industry was watching to see if the show would fall apart. *Coast-to-Coast* was a single host's creation with Alan Corbeth the creating producer. Could such a show be sustained without the founding host?

I was indoctrinated immediately by the first caller who was critical of me for not knowing enough. I just asked the listeners for a chance, and they were willing. I received many faxes about how Art would have done this or that during the show. I tried not to allow that to affect me. At the same time, the producer and the network said that 90 percent of the response was favorable to my hosting this new age show. I tried not to allow the favorable feedback to affect me either. My goal was to do a quality show.

So I focused on the content of the radio program as opposed to the developing Internet and website material. There are days where I would spend four to six hours preparing for a program that would last less much than that. There is an enormous amount of literature on the topics we covered. It was like going back to school, and I was having final exams every day.

In addition to the research, I spent numerous weekends going to conferences about the subject matter of the program. There were conferences on remote viewing, prophecy, alien abductees, the face on Mars, and a UFO conference in San Jose, where I was a guest speaker. The warm response from that audience, most of whom were *Coast-to-Coast* listeners, was greatly appreciated.

The content of the show was clearly not the normal current events that I had been addressing for years. I got to meet Dr. Michio Kaku, the well-known physicist from City University of New York. Dr. Kaku theorized about wormholes and black holes in space and the real possibilities of time travel. As a regular guest, Dr. Kaku, an eminently qualified and respected theoretical physicist, pointed out that scholarly journals in quantum physics now address in a credible, intellectual way the possibilities of parallel universes.

Other frequent guests were as follows:

- Thomas Van Flandem, a doctor of philosophy in astronomy and president of Meta Research, said that he is certain that the face on Mars is an artificial creation. That means some civilization created it years ago.
- Zecharia Sitchin translated Sumerian codes. These are the earth's first known writings, and are about six thousand years old. Sitchin made a parallel to the Hebrew scriptures. Sumerians say that 450,000 years ago, the Anunnaki came here and crossbred with prehistoric humans on earth at the time, and we are descendents of that cross-fertilization.
- Dr. Steven Greer runs the Center for the Study of Extraterrestrial Intelligence (CSETI) and directs the

Disclosure Project. He is considered the world's top authority on UFOs and alien intelligence. He recently conducted one of the most widely attended press conference ever held at the National Press Club in Washington, DC. The entire topic of the press conference was knowledge of contact with alien beings and extraterrestrial crafts.

- Dr. John Mack, a professor at Harvard and psychiatrist, has studied claims of alien abductions for years. He is the founder of PEER (Program for Extraordinary Experience Research). He stated on the air that he firmly believes there are too many common threads throughout stories of people completely unknown to each other for the abductions not to be taking place. He realizes that his being involved in this field has negatively impacted his own career due to more than mere banal skepticism from his colleagues. But he chooses to pursue more evidence because he believes his patients.
- Dr. Stanton Friedman, the renowned nuclear physicist, said there is clear evidence showing an accident involving an extraterrestrial vehicle over fifty years ago. He claims there were in fact alien beings at that time on earth.

If it ever is admitted that modem mankind has had contact with extraterrestrials, can you imagine the significance of that story? It would be the most important revelation in human history.

Some other topics we addressed on *Coast-to-Coast* were as follows:

- The Great Pyramid and the Sphinx. The mystery surrounding those immense architectural creations is just that—a mystery.
- Remote viewing. This is a phenomenon where people can actually visualize objects or places not in their physical presence. Remote viewing was supposedly the subject of a broad study by the military in the 1970s.
- Astral projection (out-of-body experiences).
- Near-death and coming-back-from-death experiences.
- Teleportation.

I myself didn't know the answers to the questions posed in these shows because they cannot be answered with even reasonable certainty. That made the shows compelling for the guests and listeners. They were entertaining as well as dramatic. My own activist-get-to-the-bottom-of-things zeal was tested because the answers were inconclusive.

At least in talk radio, where an issue about roads or schools or waste in government becomes heated, a specific course of action can be taken. The people can affect policy. An answer is close at hand. But on *Coast-to-Coast*, we considered the unanswerable.

In late October 2000, after doing the show for about six months, Kraig Kitchin (Premiere president) came to Seattle. We had lunch at the Edgewater Hotel sitting on top of the waters of Puget Sound. Kraig was very supportive and asked me if there was anything I needed. I wanted to know about ratings, and he said things were going well, but ratings weren't being considered in the first year. The show couldn't be doing as well as with Art Bell. Even I didn't expect that to happen. Kraig said the network was pleased, and that was fine with me.

Not long after our meeting, the dot-com economy turned down. All types of media and especially radio were hard hit by the inability of advertisers to pay. This was doubly difficult because commercial rental space had been leased but not paid for, and that space couldn't be re-leased. There were very few takers.

Thank You for the Opportunity

I went on vacation in the middle of December until January 4, 2001. I got a call from Kraig, who then told me that Art was coming back. I would not be renewed. I was stunned at first, but having been in the business for nearly thirty years, I can't be surprised by anything that happens.

I didn't have to stay on the air, but I felt I owed it to the audience to help bring back Art in the best way possible. I was going to get paid whether I was on the air or not, but I genuinely liked the subject matter and regular callers to the program.

The next three weeks doing the program were difficult because I wouldn't be building for the future, but the professional way to end my participation on the program was to do the best I could while on the air. Moreover, it was important to me that I did well for Premiere. The company had treated me well, and since the legend who created the program was coming back, I could understand Premiere's position.

I enjoyed doing *Coast-to-Coast*. There's something very different and special about an overnight audience. They're often very well versed on topics and challenging for a host. The callers of overnight radio, especially on a show about the paranormal, are often more entertaining than the guests.

I'm proud of the work I did on *Coast-to-Coast*. When Art first retired, the program could have gone off the air. My work, with the help of Alan Corbeth and his staff, saved the program. Premiere was fully expecting to lose at least one-third of the affiliate stations after Art left. Instead, Premiere lost less than 10 percent. Furthermore, I've since confirmed that the show's Arbitron ratings actually increased in some major markets during the time I was the host (from Spring to Fall books).

The *Coast-to-Coast* experience taught me more than just another facet of talk radio. The issues were profound. We discussed the mystery of who we are, where we came from, where we're going, what our innate powers are, what our potential is, what the universe is, how it came into being, and how it evolved. These fundamental questions on *Coast-to-Coast*, a show that Art Bell raised to maturity, gave me the opportunity to learn from the guests, the callers, and my own research.

I will be forever grateful for experiencing *Coast-to-Coast*.

⸻   •   ⸻

HOME AGAIN

⸻   •   ⸻

> Never make your home in a place.
> Make a home for yourself inside your
> own head. You'll find what you need to furnish
> it—memory, friends you can trust, love of
> learning, and other such things.
> That way it will go with you
> wherever you journey.
>
> —Tad Williams, 1990

After Midnight

I decided to take some time off for a few weeks after *Coast-toCoast AM* ended. Then spring training started, and there's nothing like baseball to bring a boy who grew up in the era of the Duke, Mantle, and Mays back to his roots.

Safeco Field in Seattle was just a few moments from my home in Seattle, and the season exploded with a new Mariners Japanese superstar in Ichiro Suzuki. As the Mariners raced toward a record-setting 116-win season, I guest-hosted radio shows across the country, including Entercom's stations in Boston and Seattle (WRKO and KIRO respectively). And I fended off requests for me to run for public office.

Summers in Seattle are glorious, and add the excitement of a winning baseball team, and it is near heaven. Then September 11, 2001, arrived. I awoke early for some reason and turned on the TV to catch the latest stock reports. But Wall Street was closed.

A plane had hit New York. The world was forever changed.

I called my friend, Stan Emert (we were co-writing *Mariners Magical Season*, a book about the 2001 Seattle Mariners) and told him what happened. The stunned silence over the phone was all anyone could say.

As someone who was raised in the shadows of the skyscrapers of the five boroughs, there are no words that can adequately reflect the sorrow, anger, horror, and dismay by the World Trade Center attack. Like so many others, the world for me would never be the same.

It took me four days to reach New York. Both SeaTac Airport in Seattle and LaGuardia in New York were deserted. I spent a week at Ground Zero. The stench was horrible. It looked like the pictures of Dresden in WWII: layers of mangled steel, other debris all over, unknown faces wearing masks just to be able to breathe.

I was there supposedly to work with KTRS in Saint Louis, KHOW in Denver, KLIF in Dallas, WRKO in Boston, and KIRO in Seattle. But in reality, I was there to just be there. There were few businesses open, but the few who had open doors were acting like family. They gave of themselves to the firefighters, the volunteers, and to the media. They gave food, rest, a cup of coffee, and they did it all with the graciousness of your grandmother. For those days in New York after 9/11, we were all family.

During the few months that followed 9/11, I often guest-hosted several shows a day. New York seemed to be calling me back, but there were few opportunities. The 9/11 aftershocks were devastating on the economy, especially in New York. But in the summer of 2002, I took a job as the anchor host for a station in Long Island with call letters changing to WLIE (Long Island Expressway). The station was going all talk and would appeal to Long Island residents while challenging the bigger stations in the nation's largest market.

WLIE, Long Island, New York

The station was independently owned and did not have the promotional budget to make the format work. I went there for about half salary and had the right to get additional work to make ends meet.

Talk radio at WLIE in Long Island was just as exciting as if I were at a station with a mammoth budget. United States representative Felix Grucci, a Republican one-termer, was running for reelection. He owned a fireworks-manufacturing facility in eastern Long Island. We had received copies of health department reports that the water near his factory was polluted. The health department had ruled out everything but Representative Grucci's factory as the culprit. Representative Grucci was unresponsive.

So at WLIE, I started the Congressman, Just Tell the Truth campaign. He avoided me and WLIE. Grucci bobbed and weaved like a fighter who had no punch. I guess Grucci didn't. He lost the election by slightly more than 1 percent of the vote despite significantly outspending his opponent. Our WLIE reports were credited with being a big part of the campaign. All Representative Grucci had to do was tell the truth about his factory.

Another campaign we did related to smoking. I am personally a nonsmoker—always have been. But Nassau County passed an ordinance that prohibited smoking, even in smoking sections, in public places such as bars and restaurants.

Judy Jacobs was the presiding officer of the Nassau County legislature and had been primarily responsible for pushing through this ban. I dubbed her Mother Judy because she was trying to tell us all how to live. Consenting adults, a legal act, it should be okay, right? The argument against the ordinance was that people would go to nearby Suffolk County to bars and restaurants not just to smoke but to enjoy the entire experience that establishments offered. Essentially it was a competitiveness issue.

But Mother Judy and her gang weren't listening. In fact, they tried to keep us from covering the deliberations! I went to the public hearing and our staff went to the regular electrical hookup used for media, but we were prevented from using it. Only WLIE was prevented. It seemed that censorship was alive and well in Nassau County thanks to Mother Judy.

In protest, we held a smoke-in at Mr. Beery's bar in Nassau County. The owner, Steve Beery, was willing to pay the fine just to show his defiance, not unlike what was done several hundred years earlier in Boston. Interestingly enough, just seventeen minutes after the smoke-in show went off the air, the police came in and harassed the owner but never arrested him.

So much for democracy and freedom of speech.

Entercom Enters the Picture

By the election of 2002, the holidays were fast approaching. I began to miss my home and friends in Seattle. About the same time, I received a call from Entercom, one of the country's largest radio station owners. Entercom wanted me in Seattle to be the main local host for a station that was going to challenge my old station, KVI! The appeal was strong, but I was under contract in New York.

Through some difficult negotiations, I was able to arrange a schedule where I would spend half the month in New York and the other half in Seattle. I would do two shows a day with one always by remote. So every other Friday afternoon, I was hopping a plane across the country. Northwest and Continental airlines and I became great friends.

On January 2, 2003, I began the 5:00 a.m. to 9:00 a.m. time slot on KTTH in Seattle. It felt great to be on the air with a full time. It didn't take long to get into the swing of things.

Joseph Leman Jr. is the son of Washington State's secretary of the Department of Corrections. He was found by his fiancée to be sexually fondling their two-month-old daughter. I interviewed the now ex-fiancée and was told of the horrid details.

The local prosecutor, for a reason that some speculated was due to pressure from the secretary of corrections, recommended a plea bargain for a six-month term in jail. I found out about that at KTTH and let the public know.

Needless to say, the audience was outraged! We started an informal initiative campaign to the presiding judge, the Honorable Ronald Kessler. The petition asked the judge to not accept the plea. Calls and letters asked the judge not to accept the plea. Judge Kessler agreed with the people and gave this sex offender, regardless of his heritage, a four-year term.

There came a teachers' strike in Marysville, a city about forty-five minutes north of Seattle. I don't like to characterize such a strike as a strike because I don't want to legitimize it. Teachers are public employees. Courts have long said that such strikes are illegal. Yet Washington politicians, particularly the governor, attorney general, and superintendent of public instruction, refused to uphold the law.

We held a meeting at the Tulalip (Marysville) Best Western to discuss the strike. The room was packed with angry parents wanting answers from the teachers. Some teachers were there. But the WEA wasn't.

The Marysville teachers' strike of 2003 was an act of Washington Education Association thuggery. WEA president Charles "Carlo Gambino" Haase seemed to be calling all the shots. If this was a local issue about teachers' pay and benefits, why would the school district with the second highest average teachers' salaries go on strike? And they have a lower cost of living than Seattle or other cities closer to Seattle.

Why, indeed, would they strike? It was their turn, according to the WEA. And the WEA knew that none of the three elected officials—not Governor Locker, not Attorney General Gregoire, and not Superintendent of Public Instruction Bergeson—would stop them.

Once again, the people lose out. No wonder so many parents are sending their kids to private schools.

Past and Future, All the Same?

Even though I have been away from regular talk radio in Seattle for several years, I have found that the culture in Olympia is basically the same. State spending is relatively unchecked. State government doesn't know and doesn't want to know how it can do better because it refuses to permit performance audits.

The governor was forced to show some level of fiscal responsibility in 2002 largely due to the efforts of state senator Dino Rossi, but the climate is still one of tax and spend: spend so that there can be more taxes, and get the people beholden to services so that the taxes can be raised without regard to whether the services are proper or needed.

The founding fathers of the state of Washington were adamant about keeping government as close to the people as possible and under as much control of the people as possible. That is why the right of a powerful initiative was granted to the people in the Washington State constitution.

Tim Eyman, the Washington State initiative guru, shouldn't be successful. If it weren't for the complete refusal of the governing class to understand public needs, he wouldn't be. But until those in government realize that government can do wrong, that government does have limits, and that government owes the people, not that the people owe the government, Tim Eyman's initiatives will continue to pass.

The people have spoken loudly and clearly that there must be limits. Too many in Washington State government are like infants seeking to push the boundaries of parental tolerance. It is time for the people of Washington State to adopt a no-tolerance policy with regard to rampant, out-of-control spending. I am continually shocked at those who place blinders over their eyes and run down the track of yes to more taxation without requiring more performance.

The coming years will be huge in talk radio and for KTTH in Seattle as well as other stations around the country who give the people a voice. Legislators and council members should be the public's voice, but all too often politicians sit in boredom behind a desk, fulfilling some statutory requirement.

Holding public office is an honor and privilege. It is the public trust. People who hold public office should go out into the community and doorbell *after* they get elected so that they can understand that people take food from their tables to pay for government services. Those services *must* be justified.

WORDS STILL TRUE, DEEDS YET TO BE DONE

> We hold these truths to be
> self-evident, that all men are created equal,
> that they are endowed by their creator with
> certain inalienable Rights, that among these are
> Life, Liberty and the pursuit
> of happiness.
>
> —Thomas Jefferson, 1776.

Kudos to the Producers

Being a radio talk-show host can be quite glamorous. A good voice, timing, and passion for issues will take you a long way.

But what many listeners don't know is how hard the producers work in arranging the shows. One producer who does a particularly fine job is Alan Corbeth, former senior vice president of Premiere Radio Networks and producer of *Coast-to-Coast*. In the ten months we worked together, I was amazed at his ideas for topics, number and quality of guests he could schedule, and his understanding of the listening audience. The next time you listen to a talk radio show that you like, send a note to the producer. He or she likely had a big hand in making it a good-quality show.

Future of Talk radio

Radio is a great medium of communications. It's instantaneous. It's easy to receive. It's topical.

Yet radio is limited in that it is not interactive for all. It goes away once the show is done; and it has no visual capabilities. While radio will, for the foreseeable future, remain a dominant medium, the advent of communications capabilities via the Internet will greatly enhance radio's effectiveness. I am working with wizards of technology who believe we have only just scratched the surface on how the Internet and radio can work together.

It is entirely within our grasp to be able to merge topical graphics over the Internet with real-time sound of the Internet. People can instantaneously contact Members of Congress via e-mail. Wouldn't it be great to coordinate an e-mail campaign through a nationally syndicated radio show? Participatory democracy is a reflection of the true empowerment the citizens possess.

Better cooperation between radio and Internet technologies will give the people even more power.

A new kind of radio is in its infancy: satellite radio. People can receive the signal of any radio station over a satellite regardless of where that station is in the world. Not only is the world getting smaller through the airplane and the Internet, but soon it will get smaller through the proliferation of satellite radio.

All of these advancing technologies will pose new challenges for production teams but will be tremendous for hosts who choose to push the cause of improving the human condition. The big winner will be the listening audience.

Why Do I Host Talk Radio?

In 1967, while teaching in Newark, I believed I could realize my dreams. But I wanted so much for my students to be able to reach their goals. Too many of them didn't even have dreams. Not enough of them had hope for the future, let alone improving the human condition.

That year I heard one of the most inspirational persons in American history speak. It was Martin Luther King, and the speech was entitled "Where Do We Go from Here?"

In the speech he was talking about the progress that African-Americans had made. He said, "Where do we go from here? First, we must massively assert our dignity and worth. We must stand up amid a system that still oppresses us and develop an unassailable and majestic sense of values."

Those words are as true today as they were then. Oppression does not come from the same place for all of us, but unless we are willing to assert our dignity and worth, we will not progress as a people.

Dr. King went on to say,

> We've come a long way in our understanding of human motivation and of the blind operation of our economic system. Now we realize that dislocations in the market operation of our economy and the prevalence of discrimination thrust people into idleness and bind them in constant or frequent unemployment against their will. The poor are less often dismissed, I hope, from our conscience today by being branded as inferior and incompetent. We also know that no matter how dynamically the economy develops and expands, it does not eliminate all poverty.

Dr. King could have easily been talking about the current issue of how trade impacts culture. One of the most important considerations where we as a people must direct our government relates to trade. The pursuit of trade is good for our economic system, but that pursuit cannot be blind. We must not bind the people of developing nations into working in subhuman conditions while destroying the environment. Being able to buy a trinket for pennies is not worth dismantling cultures.

Dr. King's powerful voice still rings in my ears, and the advice he gave should be heard and heard again, especially when he said,

> I'm concerned about a better world. I'm concerned about justice; I'm concerned about brotherhood; I'm concerned about truth. And when one is concerned about that, he can never advocate violence. For through violence you may murder a murderer, but you can't murder murder. Through violence you may murder a liar, but you can't establish truth. Through violence you may murder a hater, but you can't murder hate through violence. Darkness cannot put out darkness; only light can do that.

As a teacher in Newark, I saw violence. As a reporter in Israel, I experienced countries trying to kill each other. In Seattle, I felt the sting of tear gas in the violence of WTO. But I didn't hear people talking to each other. I didn't find a spirit of cooperation. I didn't feel the concern for a better world that Dr. King encouraged. His words were spoken in 1967 and are as true and necessary today as they were then.

Near the end of his speech, Dr. King admonished us,

> Let us be dissatisfied until from every city hall, justice will roll down like waters, and righteousness like a mighty stream.
>
> Let us be dissatisfied until that day when the lion and the lamb shall lie down together, and every man will sit under his own vine and fig tree, and none shall be afraid.

Let us be dissatisfied, and men will recognize that out of one blood God made all men to dwell upon the face of the earth.

Every day on radio talk programs I host around our nation, I hear people dissatisfied with some current event or condition. To a large extent, the callers are right. We have much about which to be dissatisfied. But until we are dissatisfied enough to improve the human condition, we will forever be searching. We must learn from our past but not be inhibited by it. That's what I mean when I say on my programs, "No regret for the past. No anxiety for the future."

Remember the advice that Dr. King gave when he said "assert our dignity and worth"? Another way to say that is the way I've always ended my shows, and to paraphrase Dr. King, "Be good to yourself and the world, and the world will be good to you."

Mike Siegel

EPILOGUE

Since the writing of this book, an interesting development happened. You may recollect a section in the book about my interviews with Father Eugene Gallagher on the subject of exorcism. One lesson I learned from that experience is that it never hurts to share valuable life experiences with others. I did exactly that with William Friedkin, director of the film The Exorcist. Since it was Father Gallagher who was the important resource for William Peter Blatty when he wrote the book, it seemed sensible to me that Friedkin would have an interest in those interviews. As it turned out, after he reviewed the DVD I sent him of those interviews, Friedkin called me to inform me that the fortieth anniversary Blu-ray disc of The Exorcist was being released by Warner Home Video. He said he wanted a portion of my interview with Father Gallagher to be part of that release. As a result and after an agreement with Warner Home Video for the licensing of the Father Gallagher interview to them, a twenty-minute segment of my two-and-a-half-hour interview with Father Eugene Gallagher was made part of the Blu-ray disc release of The Exorcist. What a nice surprise it was to see that Blu-ray disc at a Best Buy store with a cover insert promoting the interview with Father Gallagher. Lesson learned: you never know where an inquiry might lead. Feel free to contact me at mike@mikesiegel.com if you are interested in having a copy of the two-and-a-half-hour interview with Father Gallagher.

I also want to take this opportunity to reflect briefly on the changes in technology and the impact of these changes on talk radio. When we did our campaigns highlighted in this book, talk radio was the essential vehicle for having public influence over the direction public policy takes. That has changed dramatically.

Technology has made it possible for one person to have a powerful influence over these issues as talk radio has had in the past. A great example is Amy Kremer, a former flight attendant at Delta Airlines and a resident of the Atlanta area. She became frustrated about the lack of fiscal responsibility in government and the willingness to constantly raise the debt ceiling instead of reducing expenditures. Amy went online to express her frustration. It was to her surprise that a huge response from others feeling the same way about fiscal issues in this country resulted. Amy saw the massive concern in the public about an out of control government, organized the citizens who cared about this issue, and created Tea Party Express. The rest is history, and numerous other tea party groups came about. Now the power of talk radio has become the power of the individual citizen. Talk radio was the foundation upon which the new era of citizen populism and political power has evolved. Now, one person can drive public issues in ways that were not even imagined when talk radio was the centerpiece of populism in the 1980's and 1990's when I had the privilege of participating in those campaigns with the public.

How powerful is individual influence today? One simple example is the woman who was at an airport to board a Delta flight and was denied boarding because the flight was overbooked. Guess what? She tweeted Delta about the problem and within minutes they responded by finding her a seat on the flight. From that individual issue to the campaigns against Obamacare and other national efforts, social media have driven citizens to realize the power they have collectively. We will all observe with interest where this technology is going. And as this book has pointed out, talk radio was the mother of this technology and power in the people.

And how have I adapted to this new environment? I tried to be proactive as it became obvious in the mid-90's that things were changing in broadcasting. I wanted to understand the new technology and accepted a talk position at Cyberstation, an Internet=based talk network. I learned much from that one-year experience and have now been hosting a national program both on line and on radio. It is a nightly show and allows me to keep living my passion for which I am grateful.

Another element that has impacted talk radio in a profound way is the consolidation and corporatization of radio stations. As technology has grown, radio has taken a smaller slice of the audience as more and more people are turning to their smart phones and I Pads and Tablets for audio and video entertainment.

The values of radio stations have dropped dramatically since the heyday of the talk format and broadcasters are more conscious of the bottom line than ever before. This focus has led to less creativity and diversity of programming and greater reliance on the "known" success programs. The creativity is now in the social media which has taken over that role in large measure from radio.

We also saw the collapse of the economy at the end of 2007 and into 2008 and beyond. Radio stations struggled with major broadcasters reporting losses and struggles. Here was even a situation where a major broadcaster faced default on loans and the lenders were forced to re-negotiate the loans since all they had as collateral were radio stations that banks are not in the business of running.

These factors have made it more difficult for hosts and alternative options are being pursued. Hosts are making arrangements where they share revenue with the broadcaster rather than receive a salary. Hosts are also creating their own podcasts which can generate revenue and may well become the wave of the future for hosts at some point.

We have the opportunity together to watch where these dynamic changes take us and take charge of this new technology and communication environment. As Admiral Hyman G. Rickover wrote in an article back in the 1960's, the computer era is now developing and the key will be whether we are the masters of this technology or whether the technology will be our masters. The jury is still out on this powerful question.

MESSAGE FROM THE AUTHORS

We hope you enjoyed and learned from reading *Power Talk: The Influence of Talk Radio*.

Please contact us to get more information about *Mariners Magical Season*. This was written in 2001 about the remarkable 116-win season of the Seattle Mariners. This book will let even the most casual baseball fan relive each game. You may have seen some of them in person or on television.

Regardless, *Mariners Magical Season* is a labor of love for the game of baseball, our national pastime.

For questions about any topic addressed in either book, please contact the authors at www.mikesiegel.com.

Mike Siegel and Stan Emert

ABOUT THE AUTHOR

Mike Siegel has built a career through his passion for talk radio as a vehicle through which social and political change can occur. He led a campaign to stop a 51% pay raise in Congress and with the cooperation and support of talk hosts throughout the country, that campaign was successful.

When the Exxon Valdez caused a massive oil spill at Prince William Sound in Alaska, Mike Siegel asked talk radio listeners from all across the country to write letters to Exxon expressing their outrage about this violation of a pristine environment and the animal life in that area. Siegel delivered 75,000 letters of protest to the President of Exxon during a one hour meeting. Congress passed a law requiring double hull tankers so there would be no oil leak if the outer skin were to break.

Mike Siegel has a commitment to working through the media as a vehicle for the public to have influence over issues affecting their lives. Siegel sees talk radio as a connection between the citizenry and its government.

He also sees it as an entertainment vehicle as he hosted Coast To Coast AM, where the mysteries of alien visitations, ghosts, time travel and other universal mysteries were discussed with special guests and the audience.

Siegel completed his Ph.D. in Communication at the University of Utah and his J.D. at Nova University Law Center. He has been a Professor of Communication and practicing attorney in addition to his successful and meaningful career in talk radio.